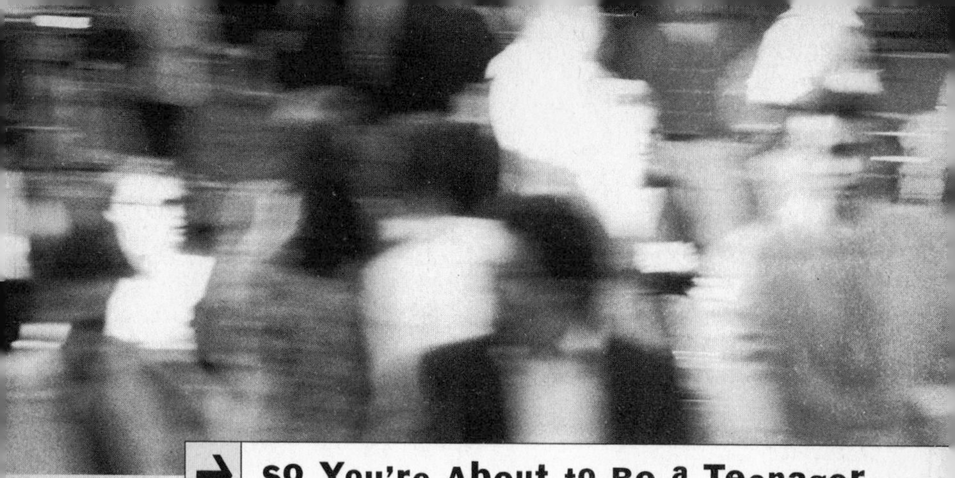

So You're About to Be a Teenager

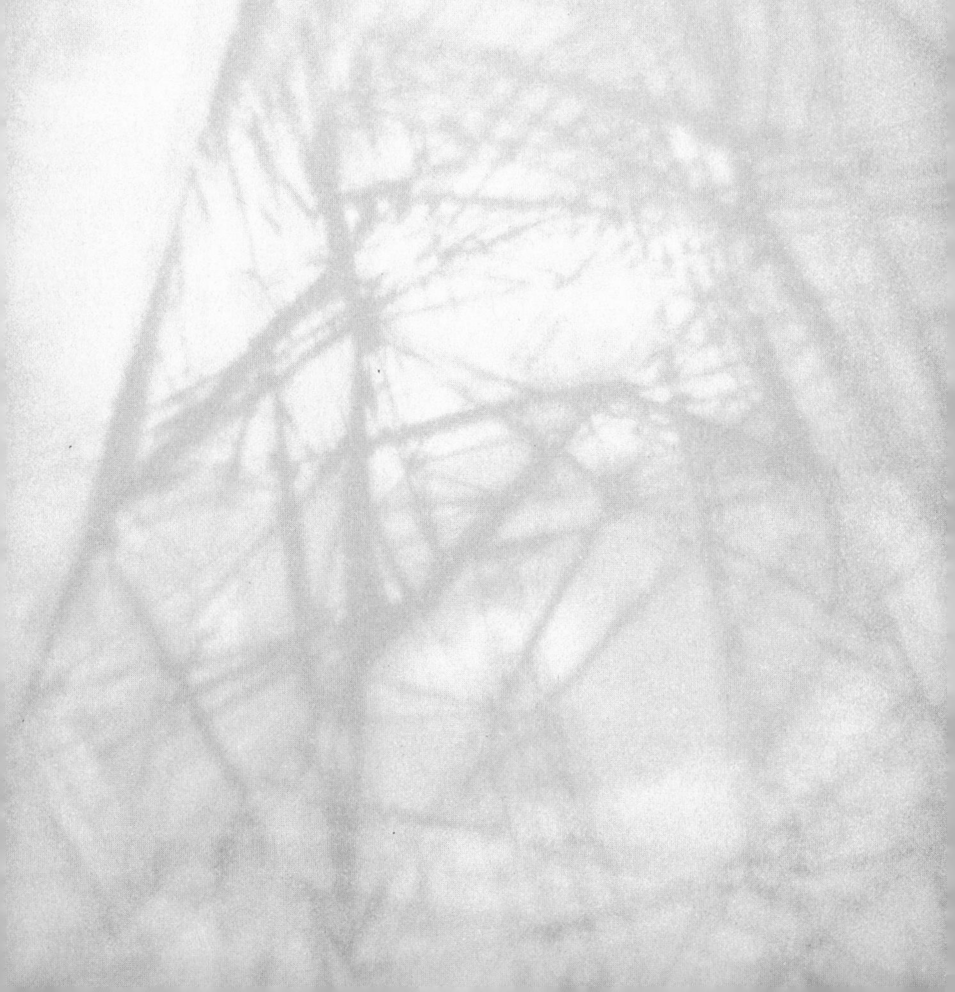

So You're About to Be a teenager

Godly Advice for Preteens on Friends, Love, Sex, Faith, and Other Life Issues

Dennis & Barbara Rainey
With Their Children Samuel and Rebecca

Publishers Since 1798

THOMAS NELSON PUBLISHERS®
Nashville

A Division of Thomas Nelson, Inc.
www.ThomasNelson.com

Published in Nashville, Tennessee, by Thomas Nelson, Inc.

This book was previously published as *So You Want to Be a Teenager?*

Scripture quotations are from the NEW AMERICAN STANDARD BIBLE®, © Copyright
The Lockman Foundation 1960, 1962, 1963, 1968, 1971, 1972, 1973, 1975, 1977. Used
by permission. (www.Lockman.org)

Library of Congress Cataloging-in-Publication Data

Rainey, Dennis, 1948–
    So you're about to be a teenager : Godly advice for preteens on friends, love,
sex, faith, and other life issues / Dennis and Barbara Rainey; with their children
Samuel and Rebecca.
        p. cm.
    ISBN 0-7852-6279-2 (pbk.)
    1. Preteens—Juvenile literature. 2. Adolescence—Juvenile literature.
3. Interpersonal relations in adolescence—Juvenile literature. 4. Sexual ethics for
teenagers. I. Rainey, Barbara. II. Title.

Printed in the United States of America
06 RRD 13 12

To Mom and Dad.
You've made our words in this book
possible by being incredible parents and
impacting both of us so much.
We love you.

〉〉〉〉 Samuel and Rebecca

To my beautiful wife, Stephanie.
Thanks for your encouragement,
support, and love. I love you.

〉〉〉〉 Samuel

To my future husband.
Know that I am patiently waiting for the day
when I will join you in sharing the rest of
our lives together. Until then I will continue
to guard my heart and my purity
ultimately for you.

〉〉〉〉 Rebecca

Contents

intr0duCtion
by samuel rainey

So you're about to be a teenager?

That's exactly where I was not very many years ago. Now I'm no longer a teenager (as I write this I am twenty-three years old), and get this—*I just got married!* Wow, is marriage ever cool. My bride's name is Stephanie, and let me tell you, she is phenomenal—and incredibly beautiful! We are very excited about our new life together.

Hold on for one minute. Let me sidetrack and tell you a quick story about my wedding. You see, when I was your age, my parents started talking to me about the importance of staying pure until marriage. Well, over the next few years, I made the decision that I wasn't going to kiss a girl until my wedding day. The decisions I made when I was your age *really helped me* withstand a

1

lot of temptations along the way. And because of my commitment not to kiss a girl until I married, the kiss that I gave
Stephanie on our wedding day was *awesome!* I mean to tell you,
it was the best thing that had ever happened to me (besides
becoming a Christian and marrying her!). It was the greatest
gift that I could give her.

I doubt that I would have ever come up with a commitment
not to kiss until the wedding on my own. My parents and others
challenged me to some really high standards. I wasn't always
excited about those standards, but looking back, it was some of
those challenges and commitments that kept me out of trouble
growing up. This book will probably challenge you in

**This book
will probably
challenge you in
ways that you may
not want to be
challenged.**

ways that you may not want to be challenged.
So, when you come across a section that you
think is off base or even weird, keep reading
and keep an open mind!

I want you to know that the information
shared in this book is very important and rel-
evant to *you*. I can say that, because it's not that
long ago that I went through all the changes and tests of
being an adolescent. Without the wisdom and guidance of my
parents and other mentors, I'm not sure I would be in such
good shape to enjoy life, follow God, and marry *my new bride,
Stephanie!* (Can you tell? I'm excited, proud, and happy.)

So, our hope is that this book will prepare you to enjoy your
teenage years. Read carefully, because the topics in here will be
of great value to your life. But we want to defer to the best
guidance book of all, the Bible. That is the single most impor-

tant book you could read to help you through your teenage life and beyond.

Several Rainey family members besides me worked on this book. My dad, Dennis, and my mom, Barbara, tackled the heavy-duty topics, such as how your body changes during adolescence, and sex. My sister Rebecca (she's in college) and I talk about some of our own experiences with friends, peer pressure, and dating. Rebecca's ideas will be scattered throughout the book in special boxes called "Rebecca's Turn." (*Why is it the girls in our family always get special treatment? . . . oops, I kind of lost my focus for a moment!*)

At the end of each chapter is what we call "Extra Stuff"— Scripture and questions and a prayer to help you put into practice what you've been reading about. Do this. It's cool!

I think you'll enjoy learning what a fun and growing experience being a teenager will be. So without any more introductions, let's start with one of Rebecca's memories of life as a preteen.

rebecca's turn

Life in Elementary School

Was your tenth birthday kind of special?

I remember turning ten and it was the biggest deal ever to me. I was finally a big double digits (10)! I remember how cool it was to actually hang out with my older sister, Ashley, and my big brothers, Benjamin and Samuel. (And by the way, Samuel, the girls don't always get special treatment in the Rainey family!)

That birthday was a big step and a change for me, but there wasn't anything too exciting going on at school.

Elementary school was a great place to have fun and grow up.

Fifth and sixth grades were okay, but life was pretty simple and I don't recall much peer pressure. Sure, some kids decided to cheat on tests, and they sometimes would try to get others to do it. I never did. But there sure wasn't anybody going around saying I should "go kiss so-and-so" or "date so-and-so."

That would happen big time in junior high during seventh grade.

The elementary and middle school years were the "calm before the storm." Looking back at being a preteen, it was easy compared to the choices I had to face in junior high and high school. A whole bunch of things can change in just a few months during adolescence: your body, your relationships with the opposite sex, your relationship with your parents, and so much more. That's why I'm excited that you are reading this book. We want to help you get ready for all those changes, so keep reading.

the box top

by samuel rainey

Does your life sometimes seem as confusing as a gigantic jigsaw puzzle? And I don't mean a puzzle that's just twenty pieces cut out of thick wood—the kind you could do with your eyes closed. No, I mean life can feel like a puzzle that has thousands of pieces. I sure felt that way when I was about to become a teenager.

My family has worked on a few of those big puzzles because my mom loves them. I suppose that's where my dad got a pretty crazy idea for his Sunday school class. What Dad did illustrates a very important truth I want to share with you.

One Sunday my dad brought his sixth-grade class a thousand-piece puzzle of a Rocky Mountain landscape with leaves in fall colors, a vivid blue sky, majestic mountains, sparkling water, and a deer or two. Dad divided the class into three groups and said, "You must put this puzzle together *without talking to anyone.*" He gave each group all the pieces for what *they thought* was the identical puzzle.

The first group was given the pieces and the puzzle box top. Those kids set the box top up for reference, sorted some pieces, and began putting the thing together. They thought this was fun.

My dad dumped the same puzzle out for the second group, but unknown to them, he gave them the box top from a different puzzle. So as they tried to sort the pieces, they were looking at the wrong puzzle picture! Of course, they could not talk to each other or even ask my dad if something was wrong.

Figuring out your life may seem like putting together a big puzzle without a box top.

The third group had it the worst. My dad spilled out the pieces and left them without a box top. Several kids broke the no-talk rule and complained, "Mr. Rainey! This isn't fair!" But he simply reminded them that there was to be no talking.

Now you may think my dad is kind of weird or even mean, but he was doing this to teach the class something very important about life.

The first group worked enthusiastically and fit many puzzle pieces together in the allotted time. The second group was frustrated, confused, and a bit angry. Slowly, each person in that group figured out that the box top did not match the puzzle. One boy threw the box top outside of the group because it was distracting and frustrating everyone. A girl pointed an accusing finger at the box lid and the pieces, but Dad just smiled and said, "S-h-h-h-h. No talking."

The third group was a disaster—no signs of teamwork or progress. They had no excitement for this project. Each person just sat there playing with a pile of pieces. This group gave up working on the puzzle because they had no hope.

After ten minutes my dad brought the experiment to a halt. Here's the point he made that I want to share with you: The box top is essential in working a jigsaw puzzle—it provides a clear picture of what the finished puzzle is supposed to look like. Without it, putting the puzzle together is nearly impossible, and all you have is a bunch of little colored pieces that have no connection.

When you start to experience all the changes of adolescence, figuring out your life may seem like putting together a big puzzle without a box top. My question is, Just what will you use for the "box top"? What picture will you look at as you fit your life together? You certainly will need one to make it through this part of your life.

Hang with me. In this chapter I'm going to tell you about a box top that will help you understand what your life—a great life—should look like. During your teen years you can have so much fun, avoid boredom, have super relationships, and experience joy instead of shame and guilt. But first you must know the box top Maker.

rebecca's turn

The First Day of Junior High

Starting junior high in the seventh grade was a major moment in my life. These weren't just the sixth graders that I knew from my old school moving to Robinson Junior High, but many students from other elementary schools were going there too. That meant I would meet new people and not just be with my little group of friends anymore.

I'll never forget the first day of junior high. I wore glasses, and one boy I liked called them bifocals. They weren't bifocals! They were regular glasses, but I was so embarrassed. Later, instead of going home right after school like the other kids, my brother Benjamin forgot to come and pick me up. So here I was at the end of my first day at junior high—sitting outside, feeling a little nerdy, waiting, and waiting, and waiting. I hoped every day of junior high would not make me feel kind of different or weird. But it was exciting—I sure didn't want to go back to elementary school!

> **I'll never forget the first day of junior high.**

Meet the Box Top Maker

It's probably not too hard for you to believe in God. I mean, when you consider the beauty of nature and the incredible complexity of our bodies, it would take quite a stretch to think all of this just happened by chance.

But even if believing in God is not that hard, it can be more difficult to believe that God takes a personal interest in our lives. You may say, "Why would God care about me? I'm not famous. I'm just a kid. Does such an awesome Creator of the universe have time for me?"

Well, yes! He is *God* after all! That means He has a tremendous ability to keep track of everything, including all that you and I do and even think. Because God is all-knowing, He has a plan for you that will perfectly fit who you are, and He wants to use you to accomplish His plans on earth—both His grand plans and His specific plans for you.

The Bible says that God has even numbered each hair on our heads! Can you imagine keeping track of your own hair that way—to say nothing of numbering the hairs of billions of other people? The total number of hairs on each head must be huge, and I bet the exact number changes every day. And counting hairs is not God's only task. Let's face it—He is *awesome!*

God knows everything all the time, and that means He knows everything about you. Oooh, that could be good or bad! Actually, it's very good if we are in a relationship with Him.

And that's another very cool deal. He wants to know us, and He wants us to have a close friendship with Him! Let's think of it this way. You know your mom and dad because you are around them, right? You know when your mom and dad get upset at things you do, and you know when they are proud of you. God is the same way. In fact, He even refers to Himself many times as our Father in heaven. But if He knows us so well and wants us to know Him, how is that going to happen?

This brings me back to the box top analogy. If God created you but your life seems like a puzzle, then who do you suppose has the box top? Yup, God certainly does.

Understanding GOd's Box Top

Let's look at a few verses in God's Word, the Bible, that explain God's box top and how it relates to you. When God made the first man and woman, Adam and Eve, and put them in a beautiful garden, everything was perfect. These two had a great relationship with each other and with God; He actually walked in the Garden with them and they all talked.

Would you be willing to DIE for people you had never met so that they could LIVE?

But then an ugly thing happened. Adam and Eve disobeyed God by eating fruit from the one tree He had told them to absolutely avoid. This disobedience was given a name, a tiny word that is still a huge problem: *Sin*. The word *sin* means to "miss the mark" or to "mess up." This messing up by

Adam and Eve meant they could no longer have easy access to God. That was their punishment. Since God is pure and holy, He hates sin. So Adam and Eve were separated from God and had to leave the Garden. This event is called the "fall of man" (see Gen. 3).

So God and Adam and Eve did not enjoy any more of those nice, friendly walks in the Garden. And because each one of us is a distant relative of Adam and Eve and we mess up, or sin, like they did, we also are separated from God. In Romans 3:23 the Bible says that we have all sinned and fallen short of God's glory. The most horrible result of sin, if it is not taken care of, is that any of us could die and end up in permanent separation from God in a place called hell. Trust me, you do not want to end up in hell.

The book of Romans also says, "The wages of sin is death" (Rom. 6:23)! That's what I'm talking about. Wages are what you get when you do something. It's like an allowance for doing chores or a check for doing a job. The payment for sinning is death.

But hold on, here comes the good part! If you read the rest of Romans 6:23, you find that there is something that God has offered to us to get rid of those wages of sin: "The free gift of God is eternal life."

How did God clean up the mess made by Adam and Eve in the Garden? He sent a gift! This gift was none other than His Son, Jesus. Jesus was able to take care of our sin problem in our relationship with God. You may or may not know a lot about Jesus, but the most important thing to know is this: Jesus came to the earth to save people like you and me from the death we have earned (the wages) by not being perfect—by sinning.

Here's what the Bible says about why God sent His Son: "For God so loved the world, that He gave His only begotten Son, that whoever believes in Him should not perish, but have eternal life" (John 3:16).

Isn't that awesome? Would you be willing to die for people you had never met so that they could live? They would never thank you in person, and they might not even admit you had given your life for them. God is telling us that He loved us so, so, so, so much that He gave His one and only Son to die for you and me! Why? So that we can have our relationship with God and never have to go to that awful place called hell. This is *salvation*.

Wow, God offers to give us a gift of eternal life despite the fact that we are sinful and have earned the wages, or payment, of death. Eternal life is life that lasts forever. You and I can live a billion years and we'll just be getting started! Now this eternal life begins while we are alive here on earth, but it continues forever in a beautiful place called heaven. That's where God has His permanent home and where everything is perfect—the opposite of hell, where everything is imperfect.

Meeting Jesus in Person

So how does someone receive this gift of salvation from God? Maybe you already are a follower of Jesus (a Christian) yourself, but please don't skip this section. God wants you to tell others how they can get their free gift too.

In order to receive the gift, you must know Jesus and understand what He has done for you. Suppose you died in a car wreck and suddenly found yourself standing before God. What if He said, "Why should I allow you into My kingdom?" What would be your answer?

It's quite simple. Jesus died for our sins because He loves us so much. He wants us to have the gift of salvation. All we have to do is believe in Him and what He did for us, and ask Him to forgive us and be King in our lives. We must turn over control of our lives to Jesus so that He becomes our leader.

If you would like to ask Christ to forgive you of your sins, why don't you ask your parents, an older brother or sister, or a friend who knows Jesus to pray with you? If you don't have anyone to do this with you, here's a prayer you can pray to God on your own:

Dear God, I am a sinner. I know that I am not perfect and I know that You are perfect. Thank You for sending Your Son to die for my sins. Thank You for loving me. By faith I believe that Jesus is the Son of God and rose from the grave to conquer death. Will You please forgive me of my sins and will You be the King of my life? Thank You for Your sacrifice, Your forgiveness, and for the eternal life I now have because of You. I will place my trust and faith in You and allow You to be the Lord and Master of my life. In Jesus' name, Amen.

If you just prayed that prayer, welcome into the kingdom of God! I hope you understand what you asked God to do, and I

urge you to please tell someone about your decision concerning Christ. From now on you belong to Him. You are a child of
God. Obey and follow Jesus Christ every day. Your life will never
be the same.

The New Box Top

I'm glad that you understand what Christ did for you. Through
His truth in the Bible, the guidance of the Holy Spirit, and the
wisdom of others who follow Christ, God will help you see the
purpose of your life and will guide you every step of the way.
He also will *never* leave you. Now that doesn't mean you won't
have hard times, but "God is faithful, who will not allow you to
be tempted beyond what you are able, but with the temptation
will provide the way of escape also, that you may be able to
endure it" (1 Cor. 10:13).

Now do you understand the importance of God being the
box top in your life? I hope that you will live by His instructions
and leading. God knows what is going to happen in the future
and we don't. He can lead you to make wise decisions instead
of wrong decisions that will haunt you in the future.

Your life does not have to be a puzzle. Let God reveal His special box top designed just for you!

rebecca's turn

The Sixth-Grade Sunday School Class

I have a few stories of my own to tell about being in my dad's sixth-grade Sunday school class. I did learn a lot, and even though I was his daughter, Dad didn't treat me differently from the other kids.

He liked using objects—such as animal traps!—and illustrations to help us remember things. One time he talked about how bad R-rated movies could be for us. He brought in a couple of boxes he had decorated to make his point.

The first cardboard box was covered with the glitzy photos of cool people you'd see in a teen magazine. This box represented an R-rated movie. On another box Dad had taped pictures of cuddly animals, cute cartoons, and photos of families. That box represented a G-rated movie.

From where we all sat in the class no one could tell what was inside either of the boxes. Like everyone else, I thought that the R-rated movie (box) looked much more cool and appealing than the G-rated movie (box).

Then Dad gave each of us a ticket and told us that we had the choice of choosing one of the two "movies" to look at, and he asked for two volunteers—one to be first to see the R-rated movie and the other to see the G-rated movie.

I'll never forget what happened. A guy jumped up and ran to see the R-rated movie inside the box. A girl who said she wanted to see the movie inside the G-rated box quickly joined him. Now remember, all we could see was the outside of the boxes and the faces of these two classmates.

The boy went first. Dad held the box very close to his face so that when he opened it the guy really wouldn't miss anything. Slowly the top opened and the boy nearly gagged. His face contorted and he yelled, "Gross! Man, that's terrible. Yuck!" He stepped back to watch the girl look at her G-rated movie. When Dad opened the lid her face brightened and she broke into this huge grin and said, "Oooh, that is cool! That is really cool!" She kept on smiling and looking into the box.

Then Dad asked the rest of the class (there were about sixty-five of us) to line up in front of the movie they wanted to see. And do you know what happened? Only a few lined up to see the G-rated movie. After seeing this guy nearly puke, and seeing the girl with a big smile on her face, the majority still wanted to look at that R-rated movie!

Now I'll tell you what was in those two boxes.

At our home we put our throwaway food in a leftover

food bucket, which eventually is dumped on a compost pile. After the food decays, my mom uses it as fertilizer for her plants.

The stuff in the bucket is yucky—grapefruit rinds, coffee grounds, and all kinds of rotting food. My dad had taken that awful food from home and put it in that R-rated movie box. It smelled bad. It was moldy and disgusting and gross! But with the lid on that box shut tight, the smell did not get out.

Have you ever realized that a lot of what we SEE in movies and on TV is just stinky garbage?

Inside the box with the G-rated movie Dad had placed a brand-new, crisp one-hundred-dollar bill.

After everybody had looked in the boxes, Dad explained that the leftover food was like an R-rated movie that has sex, violence, and bad language in it. He asked us why so many in the class had still wanted to go see that "movie" when they saw the response of their friend. Nearly everybody said that they were curious about what was so gross in the "movie."

That was exactly what Dad wanted us to learn.

Moviemakers of R-rated films will appeal to our curiosity to get us to come and see their garbage. Why would we want to watch something like that?

That illustration will always stick in my mind. And I don't think the others in class that day will forget it either.

Have you ever realized that a lot of what we see in movies and on TV is just stinky garbage? It just points out one more reason why we need the right box top so that we can make the right choices as we go through our teen years.

Extra Stuff

KEY SCRIPTURE

John 3:16: "For God so loved the world, that He gave His only begotten Son, that whoever believes in Him should not perish, but have eternal life."

QUESTIONS

1. Do you recall some of the details about when you met the "box top Maker"—Jesus Christ? If you do not think you have ever accepted Jesus as your personal Lord and Savior, would you like to pray and do that now? (If necessary, use the prayer in this chapter.)

2. What book is a great "box top" for helping you understand your life and how to live successfully?

3. If you had been in Mr. Rainey's Sunday school class on the day each person in the class decided whether to look in the R-rated movie box or the G-rated movie box, which one do you think you would have chosen? Why?

→ **PRAYER**

Thank You for loving me enough to send Jesus to die for me so I could know You and have eternal life. Help me to remember that the Bible will always be my "box top" to understand life and know how to obey and please You. In Jesus' name, Amen.

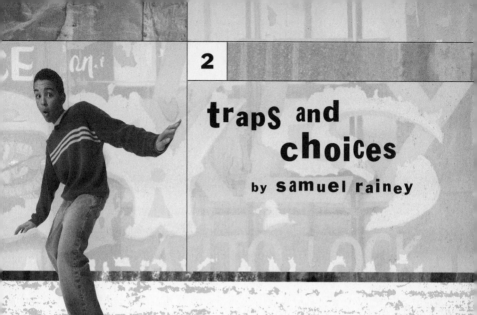

traps and choices

by samuel rainey

The boys crossed the creek and charged up
the hill, stopping at the fence that surrounded the abandoned
house. Josh, who was a little slower than the others, arrived
last. Still catching his breath, Josh said, "Come on, guys, why
are we up here? Allen's mom told us to stay away from this
place. I don't think we should be here."

The three other boys laughed. "It's broad daylight; what're
you scared of?" Jimmy asked. "We've been waiting for a chance
to explore the inside of this house. Now's the time!"

"Yeah," Allen said to Josh, "my mom doesn't know what she's
talking about! Josh, you're always the one holding us back.
There isn't anything wrong with going in this old house.
Besides, who knows what we might find or what we might be

*able to break for fun. No one will know; it'll be our little
secret. Come on, lighten up!"*

*Now Josh felt stupid, but he also wondered what he would
do if the other boys actually entered the house. Allen's mom
had warned that it was a rotten old house and could be really
dangerous. Josh was still thinking about his choices when the
other boys jumped the fence and ran toward the house. Josh
hesitated, then he jumped the fence, too, and quickly caught
up with the others just as they pushed open the door.*

Can you understand how Josh felt? Have you ever been in a
spot like that? I certainly have. Josh faced a hard choice. He
knew that Allen's mother had warned against climbing the
fence and going into the house. But his friends said it was no
big deal. Josh didn't want to miss out on some excitement—or
worse—feel weird. That's why he gave in.

Do you think he did the right thing? What would you have done
if you were Josh? Would you have jumped the fence, knowing that
you weren't supposed to but eager not to be left out? Or would
you have stayed behind and let the others make fun of you?

In the next few years of your life you will face many situations and choices like the one Josh faced. You will need to make
good decisions. Do you think you are ready?

Time to Change

Adolescence is an awesome time in life, but it can be a bit
strange. When you're still a child, most of the time everything

is the same. You get up in the morning. You have a bowl of cereal. You go to school. You play with your friends. You do your homework. You watch some TV. You go to bed. Some days are more exciting than others, such as when you get to spend the night at a friend's house and stay up all night telling scary stories and funny ones that make you laugh so hard you just about pass out. But mainly each day is the same routine.

Then comes adolescence—hello! Life's not so boring anymore. Everything starts to change, and these changes make adolescence so challenging. Your body is changing, sprouting hair in odd spots. The way you think is changing—such as suddenly being attracted to the opposite sex. As a boy I remember my voice was changing. One minute I sounded like I always had, and the next I was croaking like a frog. How embarrassing! I remember answering the phone, and the person on the other line thought I was a girl. I so wanted a deep voice.

And it's not just you. All your friends are changing, too, and sometimes they act really strange. One day your best friend may start acting like he or she doesn't even want to talk to you anymore. And that hurts. It feels like everything around you is different.

Maybe being a younger child wasn't so bad after all! But the thought of becoming a teenager and having more freedom definitely sounds better than going back to being little. Growing up is "puzzling" (sorry, I couldn't pass that one up) and that's exciting too.

And then there are the parents. I have a little secret to share with you: When I was about thirteen, I really thought my dad and mom had started taking pills that made them kind of, ah, dumb. I thought, *They really are getting old—they are losing it.* Of course I didn't tell them that, but I was suspicious. In fact for the next five to seven years I thought they were seriously out of touch with life. But when I got to college I realized that my parents weren't so dumb after all!

When I was about thirteen, I really thought my dad and mom had started taking PILLS that made them kind of, ah, DUMB.

Well, now I have a confession to share . . . and man is this one important! I realized it was I who was changing, not my parents! Adolescence does that to you. All the changes in your body and the stress you feel from those changes can mess with your mind. If you aren't careful you can lose perspective on why God gave you parents—you may start to think you know better than they do. Your parents aren't perfect and they will make mistakes, but they aren't your enemies.

Many adolescents, like Josh's buddies, think that moms and dads don't know what they are talking about. So, I hope that when you think your parents are starting to take "dumb pills," you'll remember what I learned: It's not your parents who are changing, it's you!

It's fun to grow up, but being a teenager can be very dangerous too. Many people, including some who say they are your "friends" but aren't, don't really care about you. They will mess you up if you're not careful. Some teens are so self-centered that they will trick and pressure others to do something wrong just so they can laugh at their mistakes. It's really sad. They will use what I call "traps" to snare you and get you to make bad decisions.

rebecca's turn

Friends in Junior High

Although I made new friends in junior high, I still kept most of my old friends from elementary school. I had two best girlfriends whom I'd known since second grade, and we stayed best friends through junior high. And, starting in junior high, I had lots of guy friends too. For me, junior high was a lot of fun: cheering at ball games, changing classes, joining clubs, and attending a few school dances.

My group of friends stayed pretty much the same until my first year in high school. That's when I noticed we started to divide. Many of my friends started doing things that I did not agree with. Some of them started drinking, and the ones who were "couples" were doing more than just holding hands between classes.

Because of my moral standards and the way I had been raised by my parents, I no longer felt comfortable with this group of friends. I still liked all these girls and guys—we'd been friends for years. It hurt not to be included in their conversations, and I felt pressure to join in the things they were doing to feel a part of them again. But despite this hardship, something else happened that year.

The best thing about tenth grade was that I became

close friends with a new girl at my school, a Christian who walked the walk as well as talked the talk. Since most of my friends went to church, they all thought they were Christians. But my new friend lived up to Christian standards. She was a great influence on me, and still is to this day.

The Backyard Trapper

I was fortunate to grow up in a rural area filled with wildlife near Little Rock, Arkansas. As a boy I was always out in the backyard catching lizards or at a lake catching fish. It was cool. In the winter I even trapped birds in our screened porch, but I always let them go.

One Christmas my dad gave my brother and me a big steel boxlike trap. It was large enough to catch squirrels, opossums, or even raccoons! We had the best time baiting that trap with food and coming back the next day to see what we'd caught. Often a very much alive, snarling animal was in there! We had fun doing it, but we let the critters go in the end.

Even though we were kind to the animals, I'm sure it wasn't much fun for them. And I don't think getting caught in some kind of trap would be much fun for you or me. Adolescence is great, but it can become an awful experience if you don't know how to avoid traps.

Mission Possible

To help you understand how to avoid traps, let's do a little day-dreaming. Suppose it's a sunny summer day and you've just walked through a grassy field of wildflowers. The air smells sweet, and butterflies are soaring on a gentle breeze that keeps you perfectly comfortable. At the edge of the field you find a gate that guards a path that goes into a heavy forest. Resting on a gatepost are a tape player, headphones, and a blindfold.

Curious person that you are, you look around sneakily to see if the owner of the tape machine is nearby, but it appears you are alone. Carefully you slip the headphones over your ears and press the *play* button. An authoritative male voice speaks and says your name! You hear:

> You have been chosen for a mission—you have no choice,
> you must accept it! Put on the blindfold now and take off
> your shoes and socks.

Oh no. What have you gotten yourself into? Should you run? But what if the guy on the tape is watching? You are alone facing a path that leads into a dense, dark forest. You have two major problems: First, you are putting on a blindfold, and second, you don't have shoes or socks on your feet. What the mysterious voice on the tape did not tell you is that scattered on and beside this path in the forest are a number of small mousetraps that will snap your toes. These aren't too bad, but they can sting and hurt. There are also medium-sized varmint traps that will deeply bruise and cut your feet. Ouch! But except for some scars, they will cause no permanent damage. But look out—there are large bear traps that will crush your bones, break your legs, and leave you crippled. These might even kill you if you are not treated promptly.

To top it off, without offering you any more guidance or help, the voice on the tape says cheerfully:

> Now it's time to start down the path and complete your mission. Good luck!

"Hey, come back here!" you yell. *How can I possibly walk through that forest without assistance?* you think. But the voice on the tape is silent. You are right; you won't make it safely without a lot of help.

Do you know what this walk through the forest is like? Adolescence! Your teenage years. But instead of steel traps with sharp, biting jaws, the traps you will face are things like peer pressure, dating, sex, pornography, raunchy music and movies, suicide, violent video games, gangs, Internet abuse, alco-

Instead of steel traps with sharp, biting jaws, the traps you will face are things like peer pressure, dating, SEX, pornography, alcohol, and DRUGS, to name but a few.

hol, and drugs, to name but a few. These can be just as dangerous as bear traps. Your mission is to get safely to the other side of the forest—to arrive healthy and in good shape at about age twenty. Is this a "mission impossible" or what?

Let's face it, you are vulnerable, you need assistance, and if you are going to survive and complete the mission, you must know a few facts. Today you are in luck—I have some super facts for you.

Fact 1. Every teenager faces traps. Just ask your mom and dad. About a hundred years ago—just kidding!—they faced traps when they were your age. I faced them. My sister Rebecca faced them. But if you know what you'll face, prepare yourself, and have good helpers, you can walk around these traps boldly and with confidence. You can do it because many others have gone before you safely.

Fact 2. These traps are dangerous. They can snare you, hurt you, and in extreme circumstances, even kill you. If the jaws on one of these "traps" crunch into your flesh, the scars may not disappear for the rest of your life. This is not something to laugh about or shrug off, saying, "Something bad could never happen to me." No, don't be proud. Adolescence is a tough journey. Get ready.

Fact 3. Avoiding traps means making wise choices based on good values (God's Word). We're going to show you how to make decisions about the traps even before you start your walk through the forest. If you think about your choices and plan what you'll do, then you won't make rash decisions under pressure. (Remember Josh jumping the fence at the abandoned house?) You'll avoid temptation, and no trap will take a bite out of your adolescent life!

Now What?

Okay, so we all agree you need to get ready to face the traps of adolescence. Where do we start?

In this book my parents, Rebecca, and I will often point you to your parents for advice and answers to your questions. Since we can't walk this journey with you, we want to encourage you to walk through life with your parents. We will give you guidelines on how to avoid these traps, but once you decide to develop your "trap evasion plan," your parents will be your

> **I want you to have a GOOD relationship with your parents and not go through the forest of adolescence ALONE.**

"go to" guides. And if for some reason neither your dad nor your mom can do this for you, then find a godly person at your church—maybe your Sunday school teacher or a youth worker—to help you.

You may be thinking, *But Samuel, you don't understand! My parents don't have a clue what they are talking about.* No, no, no—remember what I told you earlier about parents taking "dumb pills"? You've got to trust me on this: Your parents have gone through many of the same things that you will go through. They want to help. Let them. Talk to them. Your parents will be like park rangers, guiding you on the forest path.

rebecca's turn

My Coaches

I remember when my dad used to tell me that he and my mom were my coaches in life. Dad would always say that he was in "my corner" to encourage me and cheer me on. Actually, often I felt like my parents were my opponents in the opposite corner of the boxing ring and didn't want me to have any fun. I had to decide whether I would think of my parents as "opposing" me and all the fun I wanted to have, or as "coaches" who encouraged me daily to do what was right.

I finally believed the truth. I bet your parents are like mine. They desire the best for you and want you to enjoy life. You have to decide what you believe about your parents. Trust your parents and believe the best about them.

Your parents can walk ahead of you and help you step around the traps. But you'll have to listen to them. If not— *SNAP!*—there goes your toe. Even if you make a mistake and wander toward a big trap, your parents will be there to stop you from getting caught.

The good news is that the farther you go responsibly into the forest, the more your parents will allow you to experience the good things found there, such as independence and more freedom to make important choices on your own.

The reason I am making such a big deal about parents is that God makes a big deal about parents. In the Bible Ephesians 6:1–3 reads, "Children, obey your parents in the Lord, for this is right. Honor your father and mother (which is the first commandment with a promise), that it may be well with you, and that you may live long on the earth."

Wow, did you catch that part about "it may be well with you" and that you may live a long time? I can get into that. God commands us to obey our parents and to honor them. This means we are to listen to them and to do what they ask with a good attitude. If we do that, God will help our lives be great.

Here's another verse: "The teaching of the wise is a fountain of life, to turn aside from the snares [traps] of death" (Prov. 13:14). There's the trap issue again. Your parents are wise. They have experienced way more life than you and have some interesting things to say—but you have to *listen* to them. The bottom line is that I want you to have a good relationship with your parents and not go through the forest of adolescence alone.

I saved the best for last. Your ultimate guide through the woods is God Himself and His Word. During adolescence you will hear lots of voices (such as radio and TV, pop music stars, and your friends) that want to tell you how to live your life. The question is, Who are you going to listen to? Are you going to listen to your friends? To the messages in music? To the bad stuff you see and hear in movies? Or are you going to listen to God's voice and the words of the Bible?

That should be a "no-brainer" for all of us—we need to listen to God! But that's not always easy. You need help! And God has promised to be your Helper. If you listen to God's Word and do what it says by making good choices, I promise that you will stay out of the traps. You will exit the adolescent forest as one very cool, got-it-together person. Your mom and dad will be so proud of you—they will call you a young man or a young woman of character. And *you* will be proud of yourself.

Best of all, God will see you and the good choices you have made, and He will smile.

Oh, I almost forgot. Let me finish the story about Josh and his buddies:

> The three boys had just opened the door when Josh caught up with them. As they walked inside, all the boys watched in terror as a piece of the ceiling came crashing down in the entryway. They all ran out of the house as fast as they could.
>
> When they reached the fence, Jimmy turned to Josh and said, "You were right; we shouldn't have gone in there. One of us could have gotten hurt."
>
> As they walked away Josh realized that he shouldn't have followed the other three boys into the house.

↓ Extra Stuff

KEY SCRIPTURE

Ephesians 6:1—3: "Children, obey your parents in the Lord, for this is right. Honor your father and mother (which is the first commandment with a promise), that it may be well with you, and that you may live long on the earth."

| QUESTIONS

1. What are some rewards that God promises to children who obey their parents?

2. What traps do you think will be waiting for you as you enter your teen years?

3. What "voices" will be yelling for your attention as a preteen and teen? Why is it so important to read the Bible and listen to what God says?

→ | PRAYER

Dear Lord, thank You that I have my parents to help me avoid the traps of the teenage years. Help me to obey and listen to them and keep a good attitude. I also need Your strength and the guidance found in Your Word. In Jesus' name, Amen.

the herd

by samuel rainey

Did your parents ever bring one of those old Western flicks home from the video store? Often such a movie has a scene like this: The camera scans some desolate and tranquil rangeland, then closes in on a crew of cowboys who are sitting around the fire sipping coffee, eating from tin plates, and maybe even playing a harmonica or strumming a guitar. Then a faint sound is heard—the cowpunchers sit up and strain to hear. *What is it?* Thunder? No. An earthquake? No. Approaching hoofbeats! The volume rises. In a cloud of dust comes a herd of something— wild horses, buffalo, cattle, perhaps even a T Rex or two? (No, this isn't a rerun of *Jurassic Park*.)

Something similar to that stampede will often happen to you as a teenager. A "herd" of your peers will come storming by, and you will feel enormous pressure to join them. Another name for this thundering event is *peer pressure* (one of the traps we talked about in the last chapter). As a teenager you will want to feel accepted and admired. You will want to feel like you are "somebody" rather than just one of the crowd. You will feel pressure to belong to the herd. Running with a mighty herd can make you feel important, admired, or accepted—that you are a special part of something powerful. Don't get me wrong; peers can have an awesome influence. But be careful because they can also bring your standards down.

In your teenage years your friends will divide into groups often called "cliques." There will be friends who are a part of the "in crowd"—the most popular of the popular. You'll have people around you who try really hard to be "cool," sometimes called the "wannabes"—close to the real thing but not as cool as the coolest group. Some groups are just plain "weird"; their identity is based on being as different from the "cool people" as possible. *Image is everything* . . . you've heard that slogan before—it's the slogan of Sprite. You know what's unique about Sprite? It doesn't have the color of many other soft drinks, so it's unique.

Like Sprite, members of every group will have something unique about

A "herd" of your peers will come storming by, and you will feel ENORMOUS pressure to JOIN them.

their appearance (clothes, haircuts, jewelry, etc.), how they talk and have fun, and the kind of music they like. You will flow into a group, too, and know exactly how to "fit in" to your group. This can be a great thing. But it also can be detrimental, so be careful. I was a part of many different groups in my school, and they all had something different to offer.

You will enjoy your group because it provides a place where you feel accepted. The reason the herd idea is so powerful among teenagers is that during these years most of us feel a little inferior and intimidated. And it sure is nice to have some friends you can hang out with and not feel like an outcast.

A girl once described her adolescent years this way:

> When I became a teenager it made me feel like I was invisible, a nonperson, with no identity. I didn't know what to say, what to do. I felt clumsy. As a result my peers became my mirror. They told me who I was. They set my guidelines. They defined my standards, taught me how to live, encouraged me in the choices that I made. And as I ran with the herd, I lost my identity to that herd.

I want you to reread what she said because most likely you'll feel something of what she felt too. In fact you may already have begun to feel this way. There is a powerful truth in what she said. Can you pick it out? It's the last sentence: "As I ran with the herd, I lost my identity to that herd." Wow!

You might be saying, "Samuel, how can you be in a group of

people who accept you and still lose your identity—your unique qualities?" Hold your horses . . . I'll get to that a little later.

Let's see what God's Word says about what we've said in the past few pages. Check out this verse:

> He [Jesus] is also head of the body, the church; and He is the
> beginning, the first-born from the dead; so that He Himself
> might come to have first place in everything. (Col. 1:18)

If we don't have Jesus Christ as Lord, then we are going to be tempted to run with the wrong herd too. Jesus came to have first place in everything, which includes the friends you select and ultimately with whom you spend your time.

What I'm asking you to do now will make sense after a while. In the space below, write down the names of your close friends. I'll tell you what to do with the list later in this chapter, but for now, read on.

my liSt of friends

Peer Pressure

So, just what is peer pressure? Peer pressure is when your friends or acquaintances influence you to do what is right or wrong. In other words, peer pressure can be really good or really bad. Proverbs 13:20 explains why: "He who walks with wise men will be wise, but the companion of fools will suffer harm." How does that verse apply to you? Well, if you hang around people who are "wise" (those who make good decisions and stay out of trouble) then you'll be wise yourself. But if you hang around the opposite, the "fools" (those who don't make good decisions and have the tendency to get into trouble), then you will suffer.

The friends you choose are going to determine the kind of LIFE you live.

I know that sounds a bit harsh, but that's what God says. Later in Proverbs we read, "The fear of man brings a snare, but he who trusts in the LORD will be exalted" (29:25). Fear is a biggie in peer pressure. It's fear of what others will think, what others will say, what others will do. But the Bible says such fear is a snare or trap to grab you, injure you, maim you, or even take your life. That's why the friends you choose are going to determine the kind of life you live.

Here's an action point for you: If you trust God and listen to your parents, you will choose wise friends. I can promise you that. I'm not saying that it will be easy, but the reward is awesome.

Be Brave!

You will find that it takes courage to withstand peer pressure. Do you know much about Joshua in the Bible? He was the leader of the army that marched around Jericho's walls and made them fall. What you might not know about Joshua is that God had to command him (four times in chapter 1 of the book of Joshua) to be strong and courageous. Having courage is a tough thing, but if you are going to resist any herd that wants you to run along to some trouble, you must have courage.

Courage to RESIST peer pressure is developed in your small decisions and choices.

Courage is knowing so strongly what you believe that you will not rush off when the herd romps by and attempts to lure you to join them.

One day when my older sister, Ashley, came home from junior high my dad asked her how her day had been. She raised her eyebrows and said, "Dad, I feel like I'm standing on top of a wall, standing firm for my standards and holding to my boundaries, and everybody all around me is pulling at me, grabbing my legs, grabbing my hands, and trying to pull me off that wall. They are flinging stones at me. They are throwing words at me. They are trying to make fun of me and get me to give in and give up my boundaries and my standards. And Daddy, it sure feels lonely standing on that wall." My dad responded by hugging her and giving her courage to keep standing alone, if necessary, to resist peer pressure.

I remember feeling the same way! Peer pressure can be tough. So how do we stand up to it?

Courage to resist peer pressure is developed in your small decisions and choices. Courage is like a muscle; exercise makes it stronger. Let's say someone tempts you to smoke a cigarette. You say no. Later your parents commend you for standing up for what's right and saying no. That feels good.

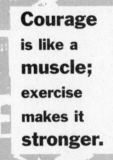

Courage is like a muscle; exercise makes it stronger.

Your courage muscle grows stronger. Another person tempts you to steal jewelry at a store in the local mall. You say no again. Your courage grows even stronger.

Now, I can't see into your brain, but I know how I was at your age. Are you thinking something like this: *Come on, Samuel, is giving in to peer pressure really all that bad? What is wrong if your parents don't find out or if it doesn't hurt anyone? I just want to have some fun with my friends.*

The Bible tells us why bad peer pressure is bad:

> Do not be deceived: "Bad company corrupts good morals."
> Become sober-minded as you ought, and stop sinning.
> (1 Cor. 15:33–34)

You may be a pretty solid young person who knows what's right and wrong, but if you hang out with the wrong group, you will end up more like them than they will end up like you. That's what the Bible says, so you can bank on it—that's what will happen to you. Bad company *will* corrupt good morals.

Either your friends are going to support you and your beliefs, or they are going to have different values and tear you down.

When I was in my dad's sixth-grade Sunday school class, he used a little experiment to show us how peers can spoil you. Have you heard the saying "One bad apple can spoil the whole barrel"? That was the theme, because Dad took a shiny red apple that was perfect and put it in a plastic sack with two other apples, which weren't so perfect; in fact they were kind of soft and bruised. He called the other apples—rotten, bruised, and bad to the core—the "two bad buddies." Then Dad put the plastic bag (sealed) in a paper sack and stuck it in a closet.

So the "three buddies" spent a lot of time together, and at the end of our class, six months later, Dad brought them back so we could see what had happened. When he opened the sack and the plastic bag, the boys and girls sitting nearby yelled, "Oh gross! It stinks! Yuck." Instead of there being three apples in the plastic bag, there was a brown soup that looked like spoiled applesauce. You couldn't even tell which one had been the nice red apple.

My dad said, "Bad company corrupted an apple that had good morals. There was nothing wrong with that shiny red apple. He was doing fine. He wasn't having any problems, didn't have any bruises. He was a good apple. The problem was he spent too much time with a couple of bad apples and lost his courage and identity." Spending time with "bad apples" can cause you to forget who you are and lose your identity.

You will be tempted to allow some bad buddies to stink up all kinds of things in your life, for example, how you talk to other people. You may feel the pressure to cut people down or make fun of those not in your group. You may have peers who dare you to steal, cheat, or disobey your parents. You may be pressured to drink alcohol or use drugs. You may be tempted to tell dirty jokes and use filthy curse words. Your peers may even want to dictate whether the way you dress is cool or not.

Peers will impact what TV shows you watch and what movie "everybody is seeing." What happens when all your friends are going to see this new movie that was just released, but your parents don't want you to see it? What will you do? Feel cool with your friends and go see it but get in trouble with Mom and Dad? That's how peer pressure works.

If you are a girl your group may want you to wear tight clothes that show off your body. Everyone else is doing it, so why not you?

If you are a boy, your friends may tempt you to look at the wrong kinds of magazines, or they may come over to your house and tell you to look at a site on the Internet that you know you shouldn't visit.

Some teenagers have even been pressured by peers to worship other gods, even Satan. I know that sounds a bit odd, but you will encounter peer pressure in all kinds of ways and all kinds of places. Trust me: Your character will be tested as never before.

Even now, can you hear the sound of the herd stomping its

If you want to be a successful teenager, you'd better be ready to courageously stand alone.

feet? If you want to be a successful teenager, you'd better be ready to courageously stand alone. You're going to have to decide on issues like: Is it more important to listen to the popular music that your friends listen to or to listen to music that encourages you to do what's right? You will need help staying strong. That's why I urge you, whatever you do during this period of your life, to not stop listening to your parents and leaning on them for help and support. How else will you grow your courage, resist bad peer pressure, and accept good peer pressure?

Standing Against Bad Peer Pressure

We hit this hard in Chapter 1, but let me remind you that *without a personal relationship with Jesus Christ, standing against bad peer pressure will probably be hopeless*. If Jesus is to be first in everything, you must have a relationship with Him.

Another thing you need to know to withstand peer pressure and not run with the wrong herd is *who you are* and *why you are here*. Who you are is somebody special and important because you were made in the image of God. On top of that, God sent His Son, Jesus, to save you and bring you close to Himself. If you have committed your life to Him as Savior and Lord, that makes you a child of God, as well as an ambassador, or representative, for God and His kingdom here on earth.

This means that as you move into junior high and high school, you're not just a teenager—you are an ambassador and you have a mission. Ephesians 2:10 says, "For we are His workmanship, created in Christ Jesus for good works, which God prepared beforehand, that we should walk in them." God has a purpose for you in junior high and high school and throughout the rest of your life. He has something unique for you to do with your life. He wants you to fulfill His mission for your life.

Before you go very far into your teen years you should decide if you want to be a "missionary"—that is, a person on a mission to help others, or a "mission field," a person who needs to be helped. No decision you make will have a bigger impact on how you relate to your peers than this choice to become a missionary or be a mission field yourself.

Back to my dad's class . . . Each of us were told we would have a choice to make on our own: Would we be a "mission field" or a "missionary"? In other words, would we choose to be a person who gets in trouble at school and disobeys parents, or would we choose to be a person who treats others with kindness, is a good influence on friends, and obeys God?

To illustrate this, my dad set up a big room that had two doors and a chair in the middle of it. Now as you sat in the chair you faced the two doors. The door on the left was labeled "mission field." There was nothing in front of it. All you had to do

was go over to that door and open it and leave the room. The door on the right was labeled "missionary." And in front of this door, my dad had stacked all kinds of tables, chairs, boxes, and stuff all the way to the ceiling. You had to crawl through and around and over all this stuff before you could squeeze out of the door labeled "missionary." Trust me, you really had to want to go out that door.

Each of us went into that room and faced a choice: How would we go into junior high school? Would we choose to be a mission field or a missionary? It was our choice to make alone, as it is yours. Which door will you go through?

I'll never forget sitting there and thinking about those two doors, those two choices. I'm glad I went through the door called "missionary," because I think my choice kept me out of a lot of trouble.

Let me ask you one more time: Which door will you choose? Will you be a missionary or a mission field? This choice is one of the most important decisions you'll make as a young man or a young woman.

In fact, why not make that decision right now? Check the circle that shows your choice:

○ **Missionary**   ○ **Mission Field**

Decide in Advance

It's kind of a no-brainer, but you will resist bad peer pressure much better and develop a huge courage muscle if you make up your mind in advance what you are going to do before facing the temptations of your teenage years.

For instance, what if you go to some buddy's house for a party and one of your peers hands you a beer and says,

"Drink this; it's awesome, and you'll feel really good!"—what will you do?

Or what if you are at the movies and a friend shows you how to sneak into an R-rated film, which is not only against what your parents would approve of but also illegal— what will you do?

Or what if one of your buddies in math class asks you to help him out by giving him answers on a test?

Or what if that cute boy you kind of like asks you to "go out" with him, but your parents have said you are too young to have a boyfriend?

Pick **good** friends (**wise** friends), those who will **"pressure"** you to do what is **RIGHT!**

What are you going to do?

Your best defense is to do some thinking ahead of time— think through how you will respond in tough spots like these. Ask your parents to help you too.

Create a Game Plan

Probably the best defense against peer pressure is an offensive tactic: Pick good friends (wise friends), those who will "pressure" you to do what is right! What a great thing that is. You need to know what to look for in a good friend, the right kind of person to hang out with.

Typically, we choose our friends—the people we will be

spending much of our time with—not on the basis of what they are really like on the inside, but upon what they wear, what they look like, where they live, if they are good athletes, or if they are in a class with us at school. We often don't really evaluate a person's true character.

So how do we select a good friend? I want you to look at a person's brain, eyes, mouth, hands, feet, and heart. Ah, come on now, stop laughing! I'm serious. Keep reading; this is good!

By looking at a potential friend's brain I mean I want you to think about what the person thinks about. What does he know and make an effort to learn? Is her mind dwelling on the right things or the wrong things? What does he think about movies and music and alcohol and drugs? How does she present herself physically? You can check out someone's brain without cutting open the skull.

Next, look at the eyes. What does your buddy watch? What does she read? What kinds of video games does he play, and what does he look at on the Internet? Do this person's eyes reflect God's pure way?

Then check out the mouth. What are your friends talking about? Good things? Bad things? Are they slamming on their parents? Cursing? Gossiping and putting others down? Talking negatively or disrespectfully all the time, with a bad attitude? What is said about friends when the friends aren't around?

On to the hands. Do the hands steal small things from someone else's locker? Do the hands touch a boyfriend or girlfriend inappropriately? Do they make obscene gestures?

Next, the feet. No, not the brand of shoes! I'm talking about where the feet go and whom the feet spend time with. Do this buddy's feet walk the narrow path that Jesus talked about in the Bible or are the feet quick to do evil and to encourage others to run with them?

Finally, examine the heart, which is the most important part. Everything I mentioned above flows from the heart. Matthew 6:21 says, "For where your treasure is, there will your heart be also." Is this buddy committed, I mean really committed, to Jesus Christ? When there's a fork in the road and a good or bad choice must be made, will this individual be courageous enough to obey God? Is the heart guarded and kept pure? Is this buddy sharing too much of the heart with someone of the opposite sex?

You can tell a lot about a friend if you check out the brain, eyes, mouth, hands, feet, and heart.

Review the Buddy List

Remember that list of friends you made a little earlier in this chapter? I want you to look back over your list and give each friend a little checkup! In what kind of shape are their brains, eyes, mouths, hands, feet, and hearts? And what about you? Are you becoming the right person? How would one of your potential buddies rate *your* brain, eyes, mouth, hands, feet, and heart? Remember what I said about being a missionary with a mission? You can be one of those people who will help someone else stay on a good path through adolescence—and be one of your great friends too. Be a leader for God and His goodness in your group.

Choosing the right friends is so important in dealing with peer pressure. It can and does have a significant impact in your life and in theirs.

Wait a second. Did I hear something? Yup, sure enough. It's the sound of hoofbeats! What are you going to do about the herd? Join it? Let it rumble past? The rest of this book will help you decide.

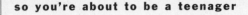

rebecca's turn

Hello, Junior High; Hello, Peer Pressure

I agree with my brother about all the pressures you have to face as you become a teenager. From the first day I entered junior high, I felt like, right away, I had to date somebody, kiss somebody, or smoke or drink. I guess I was lucky, but I don't ever remember having much temptation to smoke or drink. But dating and kissing were always a problem for me.

When I was in seventh grade I made a commitment that I wasn't going to kiss until I got married. Even then many people were pretty blown away by that.

I stayed strong until the ninth grade, which was when my parents had agreed that I could date if I wanted to. That year a guy I was dating and I used to hang out with one of my girlfriends and her boyfriend. For some reason this girl really laid it on thick with me that I needed to kiss this guy I was dating. "Come on, come on, come on," she said to me. "Everyone else is kissing! My boyfriend and I have kissed. What's the big deal?" I think she thought she would feel better about herself and what she had done if I kissed a guy or whatever.

So in a weak moment I bent under pressure. I thought, *Well, why not? Everyone else is doing it.* I gave in and reaped the consequences. I kissed this guy on a Friday at a high school game. The next morning I woke up in denial. I thought, *Oh my gosh. No, we did not do that!* I felt awful, and the whole thing was a disappointment. It was not even a totally out-of-this-world great first kiss.

I finally told my parents. That was hard. I was upset, and they were disappointed, but they said they understood. They were sad I had made a commitment and broken it.

Extra Stuff

KEY SCRIPTURE

Colossians 1:18: "He is also head of the body, the church; and He is the beginning, the first-born from the dead; so that He Himself might come to have first place in everything."

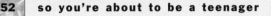

QUESTIONS

1. What signs of peer pressure have you already seen at grade school or junior high, for example, with things like clothes, shoes, haircuts, music?

2. Can you think of some situation you may face where you are afraid you might find it hard to resist bad peer pressure?

3. How did each of your friends rate when you examined their brains, eyes, mouths, hands, hearts, and feet?

4. How do you think you can keep your friends who are a good influence on you? How could you find other friends who would be a good influence on you?

↓ PRAYER

Dear Lord, thank You that You are my very best friend and will never leave me alone. Please help me find and keep good friends who will help keep me away from evil and bad choices. Help me to be a good friend in the same way to them. In Jesus' name, Amen.

for girls Only

changing and growing up

by **barbara rainey**

Did you know that as your body prepares for adolescence it somewhat resembles a computer about to get an enormous upgrade?

Think for a moment of the slowest computer ever—you know, one of those bulky machines built just after dinosaurs lived on the earth, when your parents were young! Now think of the latest, greatest, fastest, top-of-the-line computer you could imagine. That is the kind of upgrade that happens to your brain and body when adolescent hormones wash all the way through your system. Your body will be bombarded by hormones. This isn't harmful, but it does bring changes—real changes in your body, your shape, and in your understanding of who you are as a girl who is maturing into womanhood.

That's what I'm going to share with you in this chapter. I want to talk with you heart-to-heart about some of the most important changes you'll ever experience in your life. You are entering the process of becoming one of God's finest creations—a woman!

The First Sign of the "Upgrade"

One of the very first signs that your body is entering adolescence is that your breasts will begin to change.

This is the first and most noticeable outward sign that your body is transforming from a little girl's to a woman's. Most girls look forward to this happening, although some don't because they aren't ready for the responsibility of being a grown-up. That's okay. The changing of your body is a long process, and there's plenty of time to adjust to being a teenager and then to an adult.

One of my daughters came to me one day when she was in sixth or seventh grade and said she was afraid something was wrong with her. "I have a little lump under one of my breasts," she said. I could tell she was worried. Just to be safe, we scheduled a visit to the pediatrician who told her that her breasts were starting to grow and that the little lump was called a breast bud. In time her other breast also

Every girl has her own unique schedule for transitioning into the woman who is programmed in her body.

developed a breast bud, and they both began to grow larger and rounder.

I remember anticipating changes in my body when I was a girl, and my daughters have too. You may have wanted this to happen for a long time. You may have friends who are developing and already wear a bra. At school everybody seems to notice which girls are the first to wear bras. Sometimes those girls are embarrassed and feel self-conscious, because they are "the only ones" needing a bra in fourth or fifth grade. But other girls who are developing more slowly feel just as self-conscious. Every girl has her own unique schedule for transitioning into the woman who is programmed in her body. You can't start it and you can't stop it. But you can count on this change happening.

Over the next few years, you and all your girlfriends will start wearing bras and looking less like little girls and more like women. It is a part of growing up, becoming a woman, and discovering who God made you to be.

You may not need a bra now, but as your breasts grow, you will see changes nearly every day. Your parents will certainly notice, and so will everyone else who knows you. This change will be as apparent to others as your growing taller has been noticeable through the years.

Wearing a Bra

Here's why you should wear a bra when your breasts show noticeable growth: First, you need a bra for support and safety. These days so many girls participate in sports, from gymnastics and cheerleading to volleyball and soccer. Girls are more active than ever before. Even if you don't participate in a sport, you will want to get physical exercise and take PE classes during junior high and high school. So to keep yourself from getting hurt when you jog or dive for a volleyball, wear a sports bra. In your regular daily activities such as walking the halls at school and sitting in class, you also will feel more comfortable and secure if you wear a bra.

The second reason you should wear a bra is to be modest, which means not to be extreme or show off your body, but to be reserved or humble in appearance. Simply put, a bra helps you to not call attention to your breasts.

Become a young lady of godly character.

As you grow older you will notice that many teenage girls and women do just the opposite—they dress in such a way as to emphasize their figure and breasts. I want to encourage you to not be like them, but instead to become a young lady of godly character. This is so important that we'll talk more about that topic later.

You need to be aware that it's not just your family and friends who are observing the changes in your body. The boys and young men at school, in your neighborhood, and at church are noticing as well. They are attracted to girls who are growing up. Even though you will sometimes feel special being noticed by boys, you don't want them paying attention to you because they can see your breasts. You will want boys to see who you are as a person and be attracted to your character, not your body. Because of how boys are "wired" you should seek to be modest when you are around them. Wearing a bra will help you practice modesty.

> **Because of how boys are "wired" you should seek to be modest when you are around them.**

Here's a Bible verse that will encourage you in this area: "Likewise, I want women to adorn themselves with proper clothing, modestly and discreetly" (1 Tim. 2:9). The word *discreet* means "being careful about what you say or do." So as you see your breasts develop and grow, make being modest and discreet a goal. When you purchase your first bra, ask your mother if you can buy two: a sports bra for protection and a regular bra for modesty when you are around boys and men.

The Second Sign of the "Upgrade"

Another change you will notice is the growth of hair on areas of your body where it did not grow before. First you will probably notice new hair on your legs and under your arms, and you will want to shave those areas. Most girls really look forward to shaving. I remember how I wanted to start shaving my legs before I really needed to—and so did my daughters. Shaving her legs makes a girl feel more grown up and more like a teenager.

I also want to suggest—if you are not already—that it would be a good idea for you to start using underarm deodorant. Talk to your mom about the many kinds available.

Hair will also begin to grow on your vulva. Have you heard that word before? Your *vulva* is the area between your legs that serves as the entrance to your vagina. It is an area of your body you probably call your "private parts." This new growth of hair is a signal that a hidden part of your body is maturing.

The Third Sign of the "Upgrade"

Another significant change you will notice in your body is your first menstrual period, which could occur as early as age ten or as late as age sixteen. Every girl is on a different schedule.

No one but God knows when you'll start your menstrual period, but I can tell you some facts that will be true for you just as they are true for all women. You may have heard none of this before or all of it, but just to be sure, keep reading to discover all the truth about your body as God designed it.

When your ovaries (two reproductive glands near your uterus that produce eggs) are finished maturing, one of them will release an egg, which will float down a passageway called a "fallopian tube" to your uterus. Once in the uterus, that tiny egg will descend to the bottom of the uterus where it will be washed out of your body with the blood that

builds up in the lining of the uterus every month. You probably already know that if that microscopic egg is met by a male's sperm and fertilized, those two cells (the sperm and the egg) joined together will become a baby. And that new little collection of cells formed when the egg and sperm united will settle in the uterus and be nourished by the blood that is built up there every month. Just as the blood that flows through your circulatory system every minute of every day is essential for your life, so the blood in your uterus is essential for the life of that tiny fertilized egg.

Growing takes time. Be patient with your body's timing.

This process is what causes a young woman's period every month. Every time your body is getting rid of the egg that wasn't fertilized and the blood that was waiting to nourish it, you are having a menstrual period. The blood is no longer needed, so the lining of the uterus "sweats" little drops of blood that slowly wash out of the uterus and the vagina. Don't be concerned about losing too much blood—in most girls it's only a few tablespoons that flow out through your vagina over a three- to seven-day period. Your body is just fulfilling the design of its Creator, following the pattern God programmed in you as a young woman to prepare you to someday grow a baby.

But at your age you are not ready to grow a baby; you've probably not even had your first period yet. Growing takes time. Be patient with your body's timing.

Once you start your menstrual period, you may be irregular (not starting at the same time each month) for as long as a year or two. Your first period may last just a couple of days or it might last four or five days. Then you might not have another period for two months instead of one. Eventually your body will settle into a normal pattern, or cycle, having a period approximately every twenty-eight days that lasts from three to seven days. You won't know what's normal for you until you have had periods for several years and have kept track of the details on a calendar. Then you will know the way God has designed you and what is "normal" for you.

A Daughter and Her First Period

Let me tell you a story about one of our four daughters. She was in ninth grade, and since sixth grade had been watching as most of her friends had their first periods. It seemed to her that all the girls in the whole junior high school were whispering about this adventure and carrying personal products in their purses.

After the initial "good news," many of these same friends complained about painful cramps, not having the right products when their period started, and just being inconvenienced by the whole thing. Even though my daughter was concerned that she hadn't started like everybody else, after a while she realized she didn't have it so bad. Yet she

still carried a few personal products in her purse to be ready when this event finally occurred in her life.

The summer after her ninth grade year, our family was on vacation and staying in a tiny cabin with only one bedroom and a small bathroom. One morning before we'd all dressed and left for another day on the lake, this daughter's younger sister got up from the breakfast table and went into the bathroom. After a few minutes the bathroom door cracked open and we heard a voice say, "I need someone to come in here. Quickly!" My other daughter who hadn't started her period heard her younger sister's plea and went to her rescue. There she found her younger sister looking at a red blotch on her panties. She immediately knew what to do. She found me and whispered what had happened, and then went to her suitcase to get her little bag of personal products that she'd been carrying with her for more than two years.

She returned to the bathroom and, playing the big sister role like an expert, showed her sister all her things and let her choose what she wanted to use. As her mom, I was very proud of her for being so excited for her sister and so helpful and selfless.

Meanwhile Dad and her big brothers were still sitting at the

table alone, wondering what was going on with all the females in the tiny bathroom. Even her youngest sister had joined the "party." After about fifteen minutes we all came out grinning, but not saying much because my daughter who was having her first period didn't want to talk about it with the "boys." Dad and her brothers did not have a clue about what was going on until we told them later on in the day.

About an hour later I noticed my ninth-grade daughter lying on the couch. Being concerned about how she was feeling, I walked over to her and sat down. She was crying softly and said, "I can't believe my little sister started her period before me!" All I could do was reassure her that her time for a period would come.

> You will see at work in your body the evidence of a marvelous Creator.

Later, after we'd been on the lake for a couple of hours, we returned to the cabin for lunch. The older sister went to use the bathroom. To our surprise the door cracked open and we heard her call, "Mom! Come here!" I went to see what she needed and was soon followed by my other daughters. We couldn't believe it. We were all in that tiny bathroom again, laughing and giggling because she, too, had started her period that day! The Lord was so gracious to let her start that same day only a few hours after her younger sister.

With two girls having their first period at the same time on vacation, I knew we needed more supplies. All four girls piled in the car and went to Wal-Mart, where we purchased multiple kinds of products. It was a fun time for all of us to share. By the time the evening rolled around, the men in the family had figured everything out. They entered into the celebration, and later that night after dinner and the sun had set, they took us to the ice cream parlor to celebrate the sisters' joint entrance into womanhood. That is a day and a vacation we will always remember.

I hope this story will help you understand that this big change in your life is a wonderful event, not some horrible experience to be feared. What unique memories will you have of your first period? You will see at work in your body the evidence of a marvelous Creator showing how someday you, too, may be given the privilege of participating in the miracle of bringing new life to earth.

Personal Products

Do you remember how one of my daughters was prepared for her first period with samples of personal products she had collected? You may want to do the same thing. Have you noticed the products your mom uses? She may use tampons or pads or both. When you have your first period, you will start experimenting with the different types, sizes, and shapes to decide what works best for you.

Some women prefer pads and others prefer tampons. Some girls start with tampons from the first day and are comfortable with them. Others are not. It's your choice.

Let me give you one caution, however. If you do use tampons, be sure to read the information that comes in the box about toxic shock syndrome (TSS). This is something that could happen to you, for example, if you leave a tampon inside your body too long. *Toxic* is another word for poison. In relation to your period, it means that the blood and other materials already absorbed in a tampon could become toxic and poisonous if reabsorbed by your body. TSS is a serious disease that on rare occasions can cause death. Read those directions and warnings in the tampon box!

One of the problems that sometimes accompanies a period that most women would like to wish away is cramps. You may or may not experience them, and I sincerely hope you don't. Cramping is caused by the uterus contracting to force fluid—the blood—and the egg out of your body. Discomfort and cramping are worse for some women than for others. During one period, it may be more uncomfortable for you than another time. It is not necessarily the same every single time. If you do experience a lot of discomfort or have questions, talk to your mom. You need to know that some girls and women do not experience cramping or discomfort.

PMS

I'm sure you have heard stories or jokes about PMS—but just what is it? PMS stands for "premenstrual syndrome." What that means is that many women begin to feel a bit differently before they have their period. Some are a little tired or more uncomfortable. Others feel sad. With some of my girls I've noticed that little things tend to upset them a day or two before they start their period. Usually these are issues that otherwise wouldn't bother them. They may be more emotional a day or two before or on the day they start their period. You may experience PMS and you may not, but it is a very real thing for some women.

The Fourth Sign of the "Upgrade"

Another change that goes along with starting your period is a gradual change in your pelvic (hip area) bone structure. Your hips may widen early in your teen years or later on. Just as you can't do anything about when you will start your period, neither can you do anything about your bone structure. The genes you inherited when you were conceived from your mother's egg and your father's sperm will determine what shape you become.

I'm not saying, by the way, that you are going to get fat. I am saying that you will gradually begin to look more womanly as your bone structure matures. You will look more like a grown-up woman than like a little girl who has no curves. This is just another part of God's plan for you to become a woman.

Boys

As you change and mature physically you will become more interested in boys and young men who are your age. We will talk about this in depth in another chapter, but for now I want to give you a couple of thoughts about things I have noticed with our girls in their early years of adolescence.

You probably know a number of boys from your school, neighborhood, or church. You may have played together, or maybe your families vacationed together. But as your body begins to change from a girl to a young woman, and as the boys you know begin to change into young men, you will notice each other in a different way. Some of those boys are going to be more interesting to you than others.

At school and even at church you will notice that some girls are flirting with boys. Today many teenagers are overly friendly with each other in a physical way. For example, it has become common for teenage boys and girls to give each other back massages, to hug each other a lot, and for girls to sit on boys' laps just to be friendly. Often the girl initiates this contact with the boy. The reason boys and girls do this kind of thing is that it feels good and it also feels "special" to be physically close to the opposite sex. This may sound kind of weird to you now, but chances are that someday soon it will feel just the opposite. In fact, getting close to boys may become very exciting.

If you think about it, that kind of activity or behavior is not something most people do. Do your parents and other adults you know relate to other adults in these ways? Do friends you know in elementary school give back rubs and sit on each other's laps? Probably not.

As you begin to notice a change in your feelings toward

boys, you need to make a decision for yourself. Think it through and ask yourself this question about the activities I just described: "Is this what God wants me to do as a modest young woman, or is it something God doesn't want me to do?"

Evaluate what you are seeing, what you are hearing, and what is going on around you in light of God's Word. The Bible needs to be your guidebook on what you do. Talk to your parents and ask them for their advice and counsel. But be careful as you start liking boys that you don't become overly aggressive in relating to them. Focus on being modest. Focus on keeping your distance from them physically. Focus on being their friend, not on being their girlfriend.

A Wonderful Upgrade

Many changes are ahead of you as you grow into your teen years. None are more wonderful than that of becoming a young woman. God has designed one of the most unbelievable upgrades imaginable. In fact, because of this upgrade, someday you may marry and have the exquisite privilege of having a baby.

Yes, the teen years are full of many changes, but if you will let God and your parents help you manage all these upgrades, you will really enjoy the process of becoming a woman. Whatever you do, don't go through this

upgrade alone. You need to allow your parents the privilege of helping you to grow and become all that God intended.

rebecca's turn

Too Young to Date

The pressure to have a boyfriend was incredible the first year of junior high. There was pressure to date because everyone else was dating. Everybody was having such a great time; why shouldn't I?

So in seventh grade I dated behind my parents' back. This boy and I started "going together," mainly at school. He would call and we would talk on the phone. That pretty much was the relationship—the two of us talking on the phone at night.

I eventually called the relationship off because I knew it was wrong because my parents had said they didn't want me to date. I was the one who told my boyfriend, "We don't need to be dating because I'm not allowed to yet." I wish I hadn't dated so soon. Not that I had lost my innocence, but it caused me to grow up too fast.

Extra Stuff

KEY SCRIPTURE

Psalm 139:13–14: "For Thou didst form my inward parts; Thou didst weave me in my mother's womb. I will give thanks to Thee, for I am fearfully and wonderfully made; wonderful are Thy works, and my soul knows it very well."

| QUESTIONS

1. What questions do you have for your mom about having a period?

2. What was most interesting to you in the story Barbara Rainey told about her daughters and the beginnings of their periods at the vacation cabin?

3. What do you think will be the most exciting change in your body and life as you go through adolescence? Why do you feel this way?

4. What are some of the things you can do to make sure you are modest in your appearance?

→ **PRAYER**

Dear Lord, I thank You that I am "fearfully and wonderfully made." I know that my body and how I will feel about the changes in my body are all a part of Your loving plan for me. Thank You for Mom and her support and example to me. Help me to honor You in the way I dress and present myself to boys. In Jesus' name, Amen.

for boys Only

changing and growing up

by dennis rainey

As you move into adolescence, at times your body will feel like it has been hit by a bolt of lightning and that electricity is lighting up every part of you.

You better believe it—the changes that are about to begin in an adolescent boy's body are truly remarkable! Your body is about to go through a big-time change called "puberty." Hormones that have names you can't pronounce will surge through your body. Your muscles are going to grow, and you'll finally be able to whip your older sister (if you have one) in arm wrestling. The process of becoming a young man is about to begin. Let's take a look at some of the changes.

What's with Your Voice?

One of the first changes you will notice is that your voice is deepening, but it's not happening all at once. Sometimes, in the middle of a sentence, your voice will crack. One moment it will be high-pitched, and the next moment it will be lower in pitch. This can be embarrassing, and when this happens some of your friends may make fun of you. It is not right that they make fun of you, and you should not make fun of others when this happens to them. This voice-deepening phase will soon pass, and you will be talking like your dad in no time. But if this becomes something that is really bothering you, talk to your dad or your mom and let them know how you feel. It is important to talk these things out as you grow into adolescence.

Hair and More Hair

Another change is that you will grow hair in all kinds of places on your body. Hair growing on your face is one thing, but in other places, well, that can be kind of embarrassing to a boy. Let's talk first about facial hair and shaving.

As a boy I recall standing beside the sink in the bathroom and watching my dad lather up his face and scrape off his beard with a Gillette razor. The splash of that razor in the hot water and the whiskers left in the sink seemed to be a symbol of manhood. I thought that was what real men did—how cool! So, I couldn't wait to put some shaving cream on my face, scrape those whiskers off with a blade, and splash some water like a real man!

Facial hair may show up as just a stray whisker or two. You may see a wild hair on your chin and say, "Where did that come from?" These stalks can look kind of strange. You will be tempted to let it grow, but I encourage you to shave it off. Your beard won't fill in initially and may look scruffy and scraggly all through adolescence. By the time you are in your early twenties you will probably have a full beard.

> **Each of us has a unique body that matures on its own prearranged schedule.**

Hair starts growing in other places too. You will probably notice it at first under your arms, on your legs, and in your groin area around your genitals.

With this body hair comes body odor. Your glands will produce sweat that smells more like a man's. You will need to shower regularly and even start using underarm deodorant. You may not be able to tell what you smell like, but trust me and take showers daily! Some guys do not do this and don't realize that their odor is really offensive to others.

Check Out Those Biceps

Your muscles will grow larger and become harder. You may have a growth spurt early and then stop, or you may be shorter than your friends for a while but then catch up later. Each of us has a unique body that matures on its own prearranged schedule. I don't know why God made us the way He did, but I do know this: When God flips the switch for your adolescence, the hormones surge and a lot of testosterone flows into your blood-stream to work on your muscles. Muscles that used to be kind of firm now can become really hard. Your dad, who used to like to wrestle with you when you were a little boy, is going to slowly become afraid that now you will hurt him when you wrestle one another. That is all because of how God made you and the wonderful process of growing up during adolescence.

Private Matters

Another obvious change will be how you develop sexually. Girls have a lot of changes that occur to their bodies and so do boys. One of the things that will happen is that your penis will grow bigger and change in shape.

When I was your age, I will never forget going into a locker room and having to change clothes and take a shower with a bunch of guys. You couldn't help but look around, and you began to compare your body and how much you had changed with where some of the older guys were and how much their body had changed. I was little and looked at them and thought, *Man, I feel inferior.* Well, you know what? That is what boys do

all the way through adolescence. They look at other boys and compare the size of their muscles and the size of their genitals.

I want you to know it is normal to compare, to be curious, and to feel a bit insecure. You will notice, especially in the locker rooms, that guys will joke about the size of their penis or the size of somebody else's. They might even poke fun at somebody. The reason they are doing that is because they are feeling insecure too.

An interesting development is that some mornings you will wake up and your penis will be long and hard. You may wonder if something bad has happened to you! This is called an "erection" and is just another part of how God made you. It's good and there is nothing wrong!

Occasionally, while you are sleeping, you may have an erection and when you wake up you'll find some gooey liquid on your undershorts or pajama bottoms. This also is okay and normal. It is called a "wet dream" or a *nocturnal emission*. There is nothing wrong. It's just a passing phase and another sign you are growing up to be a man.

When things like this begin to occur to your body, let me encourage you to talk to your dad about them. He's been down this road as a young man and will be the very best person to talk to.

Cussing

One of the ways that young men try to compensate for their feelings of insecurity is by cussing. Some start before they become teenagers, but the bad language really gets rolling in junior high and high school. The locker room in junior high school was the worst. The older guys always tried to impress the younger guys with their "increase" in vocabulary and dirty jokes. They thought this made them really cool. Nothing could be farther from the truth.

The guys that I most respected were the ones who didn't use curse words or tell coarse jokes. These young men had control over their tongues, and I encourage you to do the same. Don't start the habit of cussing. It is not a sign of how real men behave. And if you have already started cussing, I'd recommend that you memorize this Scripture verse:

Let the words of my mouth and the meditation of my heart be acceptable in Thy sight, O LORD, my rock and my Redeemer. (Ps. 19:14)

This is a bad habit that you do not want to start or take into your teenage years. Make up your mind in advance that you will not be one of the guys who cuss.

Girls?

Another thing you'll notice is that you will have a new kind of interest in young women. All of a sudden you will notice that some of those girls you didn't want to be around six months ago now look kind of cute. You will see that the bodies of the girls are changing, too, and they are looking more like mature women. And you find that interesting and nice too.

Relating to the Opposite Sex

There are a lot of issues that you as a young man need to begin to understand as you move into adolescence. One of these is how to relate appropriately to the opposite sex.

First, you need to treat young women with respect. That word *respect* is very, very important. As you become more curious about girls and their bodies, you will find there is much freedom today for a young man to give a girl back rubs, to tickle her, or to even try to get close to her body when playing a game.

> **Treat a young lady with the ULTIMATE respect.**

Just be careful with those things and treat a young lady with the ultimate respect. Her body, like yours, is the temple of the Holy Spirit (see 1 Cor. 6:19). That means it's a good idea not to mess around with the temples that are so important to God.

Another way you can show a young woman respect is to keep your sexual desires under control. One of the things that will take place in your body and your life during adolescence is that you will develop what is called a strong sexual desire or "sex drive." It's something that you will have throughout your adult life.

Sex drive is hard to describe, but it's kind of like being hungry and all you can think about is a juicy cheeseburger and a hot fudge sundae.

Sex drive is hard to describe, but it's kind of like being hungry and all you can think about is a juicy cheeseburger and a hot fudge sundae. Except in this case the hunger or the drive is to think about sex, a girl's body, or to think about being with a girl.

rebecca's turn

What I Wish Preteen Boys Knew

Young teenage boys can be really coarse or gross. When I was your age, I liked boys and hung out with them, but the guys could really act up, and they were always blurting out gross things. I wish they had kept what they were thinking to themselves instead of opening their mouths, burping, or doing whatever in front of me.

The things they would say were probably the worst. Some boys would joke about inappropriate things and use bad language in front of girls, thinking that it was "cool" to cuss. It wasn't cool at all. Most girls steered clear of guys who used bad language. Cussing was always a signal that something was wrong with a young man's character.

Boys would also do stupid stuff. One day a guy came to school with a round mirror taped to the toe of his shoe so he could stick his foot underneath our skirts and look up. How dumb was that? The teacher found it. The girls that I knew never respected that guy for acting that way.

I was a cheerleader and that was rough because you had to wear your skirt to school. Some guys would pick you up and twirl you around to make your skirt fly up. Do you think that made me like that kind of person? Another of their tricks was to come up behind you and unfasten your bra. It was terrible. I felt like I was being violated at school during lunchtime.

I liked the boys who weren't so rough and kept themselves under control. I especially respected those boys who treated me like a real person, with honor and dignity. When one of them would express common courtesies, such as holding the door open or pulling a chair out for me to sit down first at lunch, it made me feel special as a girl. And it made me think of them as boys worthy of respect too.

Because of this drive or hunger, some guys are curious and start messing around with pornography. They look at pictures on the Internet or in magazines, and watch movies of unclothed girls. Some guys even experiment by kissing a girl or by touching her private parts. And to make this time in life even more difficult for guys, some girls flirt and may even dress in such a way that emphasizes their bodies.

What you must do as a young man is learn to keep your sexual desires under control. God has designed sexual satisfaction to occur in marriage. Some day you will be able to express these wonderful, creative, sexual desires with your wife. What you need to do now is make Jesus Christ first in your life, and with the assistance of the Holy Spirit, He will help you have self-control. Ask God to help you to wait so that you don't spoil what He wants you to experience later on in marriage. You will not be sorry that you waited, I promise.

God Created Boys to Become Men

The process of change called adolescence means that as a boy you truly begin the growth spurt to becoming a man. This usually takes five or six years, but as your body changes you will also notice that you begin to think differently about yourself.

What you MUST do as a young man is learn to keep your sexual desires under control.

Many young men struggle with feelings of inferiority during this time because they aren't quite sure how all these new feelings and desires are supposed to work. I want you to know from my experience that it can be very confusing. That's why you need God and your parents to guide you during this time. Guard your heart and make certain you are being obedient to both God and your parents and you'll do just fine. You'll have some tough times when you have a lot of doubts about yourself, but with their help you will emerge as a young man ready for adulthood. God knows what He's doing. You can trust Him.

Extra Stuff

KEY SCRIPTURE

Psalm 139:13–14: "For Thou didst form my inward parts; Thou didst weave me in my mother's womb. I will give thanks to Thee, for I am fearfully and wonderfully made; wonderful are Thy works, and my soul knows it very well."

QUESTIONS

1. What questions do you have about the changes to your body that will occur during adolescence?

2. How do you respond when you hear your friends use cuss words? How can you keep from using such language?

3. What can a man or young man do to keep himself pure and not fall into temptation when thinking about or looking at girls and women?

4. In what ways can you show respect toward the girls at school, at church, in your neighborhood, or in your own family?

PRAYER

Dear Lord, I thank You that I am "fearfully and wonderfully made." I know that my body and how I will feel about the changes in my body are all a part of Your loving plan for me. Thank You for Dad and his support and example to me. Help me to honor You in the way I think about and treat girls. In Jesus' name, Amen.

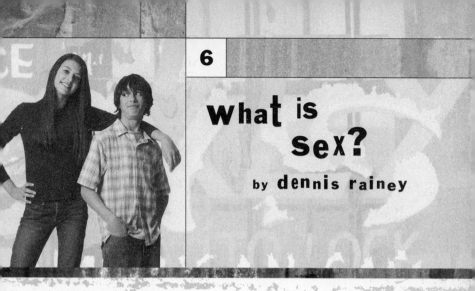

6

what is sex?

by dennis rainey

You may have heard about sex, but are you sure you have the facts? In this chapter I will try to explain the basics of sexual intercourse to you as simply and clearly as I can. Before I begin though, I want to reemphasize what has been said earlier: Sex is not some mysterious, forbidden activity that is shameful or should never be discussed. God made sex, and like everything else He created, He called it "good."

When a husband and wife experience sex, it is one of the most exciting, enjoyable, meaningful events in their relationship. That's the kind of sex God called good. But sex outside marriage is as bad as sex inside marriage is good. Understand that and you will avoid much unhappiness in life.

The word *intercourse* means "to communicate with another

person." Actually, sexual intercourse is intimate communication, the sexual joining of a husband and a wife. It is the ultimate physical way that a husband and wife express love for one another in marriage. This is what the Bible means when it says two people become one flesh. Intercourse is really a part of what marriage is all about.

God made men and women different. The two bodies, though, make a perfect fit during sexual intercourse. In her private area or genitals a woman has a vulva and a vagina. In his private area a man has testicles and a penis. God designed men

Sex outside marriage is as bad as sex inside marriage is good.

and women with these differences so that a husband and a wife could connect and become one.

This is sexual intercourse: When a husband and a wife want to express their love for each other physically, they go to their bedroom, close the door, take off their clothes, get in bed, and start kissing and cuddling. They speak kindly, saying tenderly how much they love each other. This kissing and cuddling causes changes to certain parts of the body, especially the private parts. A woman's genitals thicken and become moist, and a man's penis enlarges, stiffens, and becomes erect (an erection). At this point the wife opens her legs and her husband inserts his penis into her vagina.

After the husband and wife have been joined together for a few minutes, there usually is a pleasurable sensation that both of them really enjoy. At this point the husband releases sperm through his penis into his wife's vagina. This action is called *ejaculation*, and millions of the husband's sperm swim up through the wife's vagina all the way to her fallopian tubes in search of an egg to fertilize. If just one sperm unites with an egg, these small joined cells are the beginning of a baby. This is called conception.

God designed sexual intercourse so that a husband and a wife have the incredible privilege of joining God in creating a new life. You may be wondering, "How many times do a husband and wife do this? Only one time for every baby they have?" No, they may do it more often than that. They may actually have sexual intercourse two or three times a week or more. Some may do it as few as two or three times a month—it's up to each couple to decide. Although sexual intercourse is God's way of creating human life, it also is a very pleasurable way for a husband and wife to enjoy each other and to show love.

The way God created the body, every time a husband and a wife come together and enjoy sexual intercourse, there is the possibility of the wife becoming pregnant (if she is at her time of the month when her ovaries have produced an egg). This continues to be true until she goes through a stage (in her forties or fifties) called "menopause." After that she cannot have a baby.

Sex Is a Gift

I want you to understand clearly that sex is a gift of God and that you need to wait and save it until marriage. Here's some advice on sex:

- *Your sexuality is a marvelous creation of God.* There is a lot said about sex today that certainly doesn't give God the credit for how He made us. But the Bible teaches that God loves us so much that He wants us to protect and preserve this gift.

Your sexuality is a marvelous creation of GOD.

- *God designed sex so that children could come into the world.* Genesis 1:28 says, "And God blessed them; and God said to them, 'Be fruitful and multiply, and fill the earth, and subdue it.'" One of the ways God blessed man and woman is by giving them the privilege as well as the responsibility of bearing children. That's why it is so important for you to take responsibility for your own choices. Children are the result of sex. You can have sex and not always have a child, but the result of having sex sometimes is a child. A child is a huge responsibility. That's why God wants us to be married before we enjoy sex.

- *God designed sex so that you could experience closeness with your husband or wife.* To enjoy sexual intercourse with a person means that you know them very, very well. Sex between husband and wife is the most intimate form of

SEX between husband and wife is the most intimate form of knowing another person.

knowing another person. That's why God wants you to save this gift for your lifelong mate. A person who has never had sex with another person is known as a virgin. Virginity is a gift God has given you. It's a special gift and a challenge for you, because you can only give this gift away one time. You need to save this gift until after you are married for the person you love most, which will be your husband or wife.

Virginity is a **gift** God has given you . . . you can only **give** this gift away **one** time.

Solo Sex?

There is one more important topic where you need information from a Christian perspective—not just the world's ideas from a friend at school or an article in a teen magazine.

As you grow older you will hear about something called "masturbation" or self-stimulation. This is when a boy or girl rubs his or her own private parts to experience the pleasurable feelings found through sexual intercourse.

Some people believe it is okay for a young person to masturbate because the Bible is "silent" about masturbation. It is true that the Bible is silent about masturbation, but the Bible is not silent about sex. Nowhere in Scripture do we find God's blessing of sex in solo, done by *only* you. However, we do find that God blesses sex in marriage between a husband and a wife.

Even though the desire for sex may be present during your teenage years and beyond, I still believe that God didn't make sex to be done by only one person. He made it for a husband and a wife to enjoy together. When a husband and a wife experience sex as they are supposed to, they think about how to make their spouse feel good. But when a preteen or teenager masturbates, the focus is on what feels good to him or her. The young person focuses on *self*, rather than *selflessly* serving a mate—which is what sex in marriage is all about.

Additionally, when a boy or girl starts masturbating there is a temptation to think about the wrong things: The mind fills up with sexual images that are inappropriate. Many older teens and adults who masturbate develop a selfish habit that can lead into other things that are far worse, such as visiting sex chat rooms and pornographic Web pages on the Internet. Young men and women who masturbate and think about sex too much may make themselves more vulnerable to those who are sexually active or even to sexual predators. For example, if a young girl thinks about sex all the time, she becomes more vulnerable to a boy or man who wants to use her to satisfy his sexual desires. Some boys and girls who dwell on sex may later in their lives develop a serious problem called "sexual addiction."

None of this has to happen! God wants you to practice self-control. You need to learn with His help how to control your sexual urges and conquer lust as a young person. This will benefit you greatly later on in marriage.

You may ask, "But what should I do with my sexual desires now?" Here are some suggestions:

First, talk to your parents. If you are struggling with your thoughts or if you heard something at school that upsets you, spend some time honestly talking with your mom or dad about your fears, questions, and feelings.

Second, don't feed your sexual thoughts by reading the wrong kinds of books or magazines, watching sex-filled movies and television shows, or listening to secular love songs. Girls can read romance novels that can cause them to have sexual thoughts when they should be guarding their hearts instead. Boys can guard their hearts by refusing to look at pictures of nude women in magazines or on the Internet.

Third, stay busy. Be active, join clubs, get plenty of exercise, enjoy church activities, and take your share of responsibilities around your home. Staying busy with worthwhile stuff not only keeps you out of needless trouble, it helps you make a lifelong habit of positive productivity.

Finally, keep on practicing self-control. The key word is *practice*. None of us live a perfect life. But if you do fail, realize that your heavenly Father loves you. Seek His forgiveness and grace. Then go on— *practice* self-control some more. God will not withdraw His relationship from you or punish you if you struggle or fail in the area of masturbation.

I know this is a sensitive and kind of embarrassing topic. But like everything else, it's just another area where Jesus Christ wants first place in your life. He will walk beside you and provide the strength you need to live a life that pleases and glorifies Him.

God designed sex and marriage to bring you a great deal of pleasure. Since He created it, God really approves of sex within marriage. He wants you to enjoy sex in marriage. The danger comes if you step into a trap and experience sex before marriage, when you are truly not ready. God wants you to protect and preserve the sexual gift you have for your husband or wife.

Extra Stuff

KEY SCRIPTURE

Genesis 1:27: "And God created man in His own image, in the image of God He created him; male and female He created them."

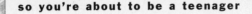

QUESTIONS

1. Why is God not "down" on sex? How do we know that?

2. How many times does a couple have to have sex in order for the girl to have a baby?

3. Why is it best to wait to be married to have sex?

4. Is there anything you do not understand about sexual inter-course that you would like explained? Ask your parent.

PRAYER

Dear God, thank You for the changes You will make in my body, which will include the opportunity in Your will someday to enjoy having sex with my spouse and become a parent. You are awesome! In Jesus' name, Amen.

dangerous cliffs ahead

by dennis rainey

Once upon a time a kindhearted but shrewd queen ruled a domain far, far away. During times of peace this queen loved to be out among her people, riding in her royal journeying chair, waving to children, and granting blessings to her subjects. The queen was carried proudly by the six most honorable knights of the kingdom, the Knights of the Courageous Heart. During times of war, these six fought with the other kingdom warriors in defense of their lands and villages.

In the most recent struggle at the Battle of Weeping Glen, Knight Vincent had died while heroically rescuing a peasant widow trapped in her burning cottage. Now the queen desired to visit among her people again. It was time

to choose Sir Vincent's successor. All knights of the Kingdom
of Ambrose were summoned to the queen's palace.

Queen: "Knights of Ambrose, I have gathered you here
today to choose a replacement for Sir Vincent. The man I
choose will serve in my court, advise me in matters of
state, and most important, bear me upon my chair. My
reputation, my honor, and my life will be in his care. My
safety is the kingdom's safety."

After a long pause to let the solemnity of her words
settle firmly in each man's mind and heart, the queen
began her selection by calling out the first of three men
from the rows of knights standing at stiff attention: "Sir
Arnold!"

Sir Arnold: "Yes, My Queen."

Queen: "Would you like to serve in my court and become

an honored member of the Knights of the
Courageous Heart?"

Sir Arnold: "Yes, Your Highness, it would
please me greatly."

Queen: "Very well. I know you to be
strong and brave, Sir Arnold, and I know you have served
my kingdom well in battle. You need only answer this
question: If you were carrying my throne around Charis
Cliff where the path is narrow, how close to the edge
would you go?"

Sir Arnold: "My lady, it is as you say. I am strong and
brave. I could carry you within one foot of the cliff's
edge."

Queen: "I see. Thank you, Sir Arnold. Sir Jared!"

Sir Jared: "My Queen, I am your servant."

Queen: "You also have distinguished yourself in royal service. What say you? How close to the edge of the cliff would you carry my chair?"

Sir Jared: "I am as strong and brave as Sir Arnold, and I possess perfect balance. I could carry your throne within six inches of the edge."

Queen: "Thank you, Sir Jared. Now, Sir Conner! What would you do?"

Sir Conner: "Your Highness, were I granted the honor of carrying your chair upon my shoulders, I would go nowhere near the edge of Charis Cliff. You have kept us safe from our enemies; you have fed your kingdom from your storehouses; you have prayed for our peace. Your life is far too precious. I would never put you near danger. The safest place to carry you would be as far away from the cliff's edge as possible."

Queen: "Sir Conner, the wise, I choose you to serve as the newest member of the elite Knights of the Courageous Heart."

Sir Conner: "It would be my greatest honor, Your Highness."

Now, why did I tell that story?

In the last chapter I talked about God's special gift called "sex"—which to you now may sound kind of weird and even yucky, but trust me, it's very cool. God gave this to you, and you can either keep and protect it or go out to the edge of the cliff and maybe lose it.

As you become a teenager, you will see how your friends, classmates, and other peers handle the gift. Some of them, like Sir Jared in the story, will get as close to "the edge" as they possibly can. They may lose their balance, fall, and end up being loaded into an ambulance at the bottom of the valley. Others may run up and look over the edge and then run back to safety. Some of your friends may listen to the wisdom of their parents and others like Barbara and me and go nowhere near the cliff's edge. Others will play around the edge and break off little bits of the gift and give it away a piece at a time. Some may just hand the gift over all at once.

Do you understand what I'm saying? You have to decide for yourself what you will do with God's gift of sex. And the best time to decide is before you get in a situation where you may be tempted to do something wrong that you will regret.

Many of those who lose the gift of sex will actually act like it's a huge achievement and even brag about it—especially boys. Others who want to protect and preserve their gift until they get married may feel strange because there will be people around them giving their gift away. These kids might even be made fun of by the ones who have given sex away.

Find Advice You Can Trust

One summer our family visited the Royal Gorge, which is a very deep and narrow canyon in Colorado with the Arkansas River at the bottom and a bridge spanning the two sides at the top.

As we drove up to the Royal Gorge Park, we explained to our children what they would see. Samuel, who was about ten at the time, wanted to beat everyone else and see the gorge first. As soon as I parked the car, he ran toward some large boulders beyond the parking area. I had never been to the Royal Gorge before, so I assumed the boulders were far away from the edge.

When I caught up with Samuel, to my horror I saw that just a few feet beyond the rocks was the gorge, its sheer sides dropping more than a thousand feet to the river below. Then, to my great relief, I also saw a chain-link fence at the edge of the rocks that would catch Samuel if he went too far and slipped.

Explaining why sex outside of marriage can be so dangerous for you is like explaining the dangers of the Royal Gorge. Unless you've seen how deep the canyon is, you can't imagine the devastation caused by falling over the edge.

Simply put, your brain can't help you understand what it hasn't experienced. You have to trust the advice of someone who knows. Understanding a fall in the Royal Gorge or sex is a matter of trust. You have to decide to trust someone who knows the truth.

Barbara and I and your parents can explain sex, a "place" you've never been. We can warn you of the dangers of going there before marriage. But you must choose to trust us and believe we are telling you the truth.

Think about it! When you were a baby, your mom and dad taught you what "hot" meant so you wouldn't burn yourself. When you were a toddler, they put a gate at the top of the stairs so you wouldn't fall. Later, they taught you not to play in the street so you wouldn't be hit by a car. Every time you've gotten sick, they've taken care of you, brought you to the doctor if necessary, given you your medicine, and stayed up with you at night.

Wounds from sex before marriage damage the heart, where we love, trust, and believe.

Now if people like that have told you the truth and have been good to you so far (even though we know they aren't perfect), what if they tell you to stay away from the cliff of sex when you are a teenager? Would it not be a good idea to trust them?

Why Do Teenagers Risk Sex?

So why do so many teenagers not play it safe and stay away from the edge when it comes to sex?

One reason is that having sex before marriage does not immediately show the damage that would occur from a fall into the Royal Gorge. If one of your friends went on a hike and fell down a steep slope, you could visit him in the hospital, see his bandages and bruises, and even sign your name on his cast. But if another one of your close friends decided to have sex on a Saturday night, he or she would be back at school on Monday and no one could tell by looking that your friend had been hurt.

Most of the wounds from sex before marriage are hidden deep inside a person. The damage is done to the heart, where we love, trust, and believe. Those with sex wounds can't trust people as much as they used to. They are sadder and more afraid, and they feel ashamed and guilty. And these wounds don't heal quickly and cleanly like a broken leg does. Some of them never heal. For example, if a boy and girl become parents of a child they are too young to raise, giving the baby up for adoption will cause hurt in the heart for a lifetime.

Some teenagers think that ending a "mistaken" pregnancy by abortion would be a better solution than having the baby. I want you to know on the authority of God's Word—*abortion is never a right choice. NEVER!* We need to always protect unborn life, no matter how badly we feel about what we did wrong. Many thousands of adult women (and the men who fathered their children) are very sad and filled with guilt and regret because of choosing to abort an unplanned or unwanted pregnancy. These decisions may have occurred years earlier in their lives, but they still carry a weight of guilt with them as an adult. Yes, it's a big mistake to have sex and get pregnant outside of marriage. But don't follow it up with an even greater mistake—abortion. And I challenge you to become a protector of unborn life by never advising a friend to get an abortion. Encourage your friend to become a protector of unborn life too. Your courage may actually be used by God to save a human life.

There are other wounds from sex before marriage. An increasing number of teenagers are becoming sick from more than fifty kinds of sexually transmitted diseases (also called STDs). A person becomes infected with an STD through sexual contact with the opposite sex. Of course, not everyone who has sex gets an STD, but because many boys and girls are sexually active, many young people are infected with STDs.

Opening God's gift of sex outside of marriage has very serious consequences.

Many STDs cannot be cured and are extremely painful. Some of these diseases may prevent a woman from ever having a child. Some of them can even kill you. Opening God's gift of sex outside of marriage has very serious consequences.

Build Some Fences!

Remember what I saw when I caught up with Samuel at the Royal Gorge? A fence. That fence was there to protect boys like Samuel who didn't understand the danger, or teenagers who might stand too close to the edge to impress friends, or adults like me who are scared of heights.

Think about how many "fences" there are. Fences at the zoo to protect visitors from the animals and to protect some of the animals from people. Fences around school playgrounds to protect the children playing there. Fences around manufacturing plants, airports, and the White House.

Fences are barriers. They establish boundaries. Boundaries protect you from things that could hurt you. Other words that have a meaning similar to boundaries are *standards, rules, convictions,* and *values.* These are all very good as you become a teenager.

Your parents will help you set some standards and establish some boundaries on how close to the edge of the cliff you are going to go as a

> **Boundaries protect you from things that could hurt you.**

young person. If your parents don't help you with these boundaries, then your "limits" will be set by what you learn from your friends, others your own age, or people you think are "cool." But all these may have no experience with the Royal Gorge or sex. Can you trust them to know what to do? Do they care for you like your parents do?

rebecca's turn

Group Dating Is Great!

When you start having an interest in dating someone, instead of pairing off, I would encourage you to have a group of boys and girls over to your house. Rent a stupid movie you can all laugh at instead of a romantic movie that will make you emotional when you don't need to be. Guys don't enjoy romantic movies—not at your age anyway. Sure it's fun to do that with girls, but when you are with boys, it's kind of different. Everyone can enjoy a funny movie.

Group activities also allow you to get to know a person better. You can see how he or she relates to other people. You can watch people from a distance. Then you'll know that "he's nice" or "she has a bad attitude." Group settings prevent couples from being singled out and eliminate the pressure to kiss or cuddle just because another couple are. Groups can be more fun and you can make more friends too!

Boundaries for Sex

Where does God draw the line regarding sex? What are His boundaries?

The apostle Paul wrote to his young friend Timothy, "Flee from youthful lusts" (2 Tim. 2:22). In 1 Corinthians 6:18 Paul said, "Flee immorality." These verses mean you are to run away from evil, to *flee* from any form of sexual wrongdoing.

If for some reason you are alone with a boy or girl too near the "edge of the gorge" and are tempted to do some sexual things, you have to get out of there! First Thessalonians 4:3 says, "For this is the will of God, your sanctification; that is, that you abstain from sexual immorality." In other words, *don't have sex!* It's God's will that you do not participate in sexual affection and activity prior to marriage.

So, what kind of fence can you build to protect yourself from sex before marriage? Let me give you a few ideas, but for sure you and your parents need to talk about your standards—the boundaries you need to keep you away from sex before marriage.

Here are my thoughts to help you stay pure.

Trust God!

You can keep your life pure by knowing what God says in the Bible about sex before marriage and trusting Him. God doesn't say no to sex. He says yes to sex—in marriage. God wants you to be sexually pure when you enter into marriage. Sexual purity means going nowhere near the edge of the cliff. It means saving the sexual gift God has given you until you can give it to another person in marriage.

Think Right!

You can keep your life pure by thinking the right things: "Set your mind on the things above, not on the things that are on

earth" (Col. 3:2). God has given us a wonderful thing in the mind. It is powerful! But we can fill our minds with the wrong thoughts about romance, about girls and boys and their bodies and what they look like, and what sex is all about.

Guard Your Heart!

You can keep your life pure by guarding your heart. Your heart is the whole you—all the things inside that make you unique and special. "Watch over your heart with all diligence, for from it flow the springs of life," Solomon advised in Proverbs 4:23. Your heart is like a spring of clear, pure water. You don't want to dump poison into that spring. One way to guard your heart is to spend time reading and memorizing verses from God's Word, to think about God, to talk to God, and to ask God to walk beside you, day to day.

Watch Your Eyes!

You can keep your life pure by not looking at the wrong things. In Psalms it says, "I will set no worthless thing before my eyes" (101:3). Some worthless things are dirty pictures showing naked men and women doing sexual things—that's called "pornography." Even many of the pictures of men and women with clothes on—if they are looking sexy—are not good to look at and prevent you from being pure.

Avoid Internet Traps!

You can keep your life pure by wise use of the Internet. When you are on-line, you are just a mouse click away from evil material and danger. Watch out for unwanted "spam" e-mails from pornography Web sites. If someone sends you bad stuff, tell your parents. If you accidentally end up at a location on the Internet where you should not be, do what Joseph did when tempted in Egypt: Run! Then ask a parent for help.

Be especially careful about exchanging e-mail messages with strangers. Don't ever reveal to someone you don't know your real name, address, phone number, where you go to school, or other personal information. Don't send your picture on-line. If you get scared or suspicious of someone, tell your parents. Many boys and girls have gotten into big trouble or have even died when meeting a "friend" from the Internet.

Control Hands and Lips!

You can keep your life pure by keeping your hands and lips out of trouble. Both boys and girls need to be careful how they touch each other. Holding hands is pretty innocent, isn't it? But what if the good feelings that come from holding someone's hand make you want to touch him or her in a more private place? Then is holding hands all that harmless?

You can keep your life pure by keeping your hands and lips out of trouble.

The same goes for kissing. There are two kinds of kisses: The first is a light kiss—maybe on the cheek—that says, "I like you; you're special." Pretty innocent, huh? Unfortunately that kind of kiss can turn into a passionate kiss in a nanosecond, the kind of kiss that says, "I like you a lot—let's do more kissing!" It's a kiss that demands the other person respond with similar emotion.

When my daughter Rebecca was invited to her high school prom, I asked her date if I could meet with him before the prom. He came by the house and we talked. I looked him straight in the eye and said, "I would like to ask you to honor my daughter. She is very beautiful and attractive, and I would like to ask you to keep your lips off my daughter—not to kiss her."

He turned kind of red and was embarrassed. It was also hard for me to say that to him. But it was a great conversation. We walked out shaking one another's hand, and I told him how proud I was that he had come to talk to me as a dad before he took my daughter to prom.

You know what? Rebecca and her date had a wonderful time. And no, he didn't kiss her. They had fun without ending their date with a kiss.

A Special Warning from Mr. Rainey!

I want to warn you about some of the little games you may be asked to play in junior high and high school. Teenagers are so attracted to the opposite sex that they create ways to get close to each other, such as tickling and wrestling, giving back rubs, or having a girl sit on a boy's lap. The problem is that these things can stimulate your desire to be physically close to someone of the opposite sex in an unhealthy way. Your goal ought to be to remain sexually pure and to stay as far away from the edge of this cliff as possible.

Do What's Right

It is never too late to do what is right. You can decide today to ask God to help you be pure concerning sex. Why start something when you have to stop? Passionate kissing, hugging, and touching in private places isn't right. God's Word clearly says not to do it unless you are married—and you are way too young to get married! If you want to make sure that you are

going to stay sexually pure, then build your fence as far from the edge of the cliff as you possibly can.

Let me promise you something! When you save your sex gift for marriage by staying away from the edge

It is **never too late** to do what is **right.**

of the cliff and holding to high standards, you are not going to experience shame and feel bad about a wrong choice. You won't be sick or die from some disease you picked up through sex outside marriage. You are going to have a clear conscience. And you will really enjoy giving your gift of sex to the one you love.

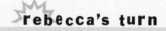

rebecca's turn

Junior High Life Can Be Embarrassing!

Why do things like this have to happen when you start caring more about what someone of the opposite sex thinks about you?

When I was in seventh and eighth grades, I had braces on my teeth, which required me to wear an orthodontic headgear mainly at night and sometimes around the house. It was kind of like a bit for a horse: A metal thing went in your mouth, and the rest of the hat-like thing was on your head. It was so ugly! I would never wear it in public.

One day Mom picked me up after school to go to the orthodontist to get this headgear tightened. After that we went to a shoe store. Mom said to me, "Why don't you just wear your headgear and get some more time in on it? Your teeth need it."

"But, Mom, what if I see someone I know? I'll be so embarrassed," I said. This was one of my big fears.

"You're not going to see anyone."

"Okay, Mom, why not." I was tired. I wanted the conversation to end. *Fine, you win, I'll wear it.*

So I have this thing on, I'm in the shoe store, and Mom is not even with me—she's off somewhere else in the store. I forgot I had the headgear on! Lo and behold, I did see someone—a boy I liked at school! When he saw me, his face turned so red. I was thinking, What is the deal? What's his problem? I totally forgot this ugly thing was in my face and on my head. Then, of course, I realized what was going on. It was awful.

I found my mom and told her, "I am never wearing that in public again. I told you I would see someone."

Of course the next day this guy told the whole school that he had seen me with my headgear on. But I didn't care too much. His face got red, not mine.

Extra Stuff

KEY SCRIPTURE

1 Corinthians 10:13: "No temptation has overtaken you but such as is common to man; and God is faithful, who will not allow you to be tempted beyond what you are able, but with the temptation will provide the way of escape also, that you may be able to endure it."

QUESTIONS

1. What was most interesting to you about the story of the queen and the knights who carried her chair? (See pages 93–95.)

2. Why is it so dangerous to walk up to the edge of a steep cliff?

3. If you have a choice, would you rather have a fence at the top edge of a steep cliff or no fence? Why do you say that?

4. Why would having sex before marriage be so unwise?

5. Why do your friends not care as much for your safety and success in life as your parents do?

6. What are some of the dangers of losing some of your innocence on the Internet?

7. How can you avoid getting hurt while using the Internet?

8. In what areas of your life do you think you might need strong boundaries or fences?

PRAYER

Dear Lord, thank You that I have parents who are concerned about my safety and innocence. Help me to obey them and listen to the wisdom You have given them that helps me. Please help me to set up strong fences, make good choices, and keep my purity. In Jesus' name, Amen.

dating?

by samuel rainey

Yup, there it is—that magical, yet kind of scary word: *dating*.

Let me turn back the clock for a moment to seventh grade when I was head over heels for this girl I'll call Ginger (not her real name). Well, I heard through the grapevine (you know how those go) that she was interested in me. Being the savvy, confident seventh grader that I was, I decided to see if she'd want to "go with me." I remember giving her a note asking her to be my girlfriend. And she said YES!

At the time, I thought I was king of the world. We had a great time being together at school and at football games. I remember looking forward to fourth period at school because that's when we would exchange notes between classes!

Well, we "went together" for about four months. During that time I had tons of pressure to kiss her. I didn't want to do so because kissing wasn't that big of a deal to me. Well, it ended up that she broke up with me, mostly because I wouldn't kiss her.

This was my first and last girlfriend before I met Stephanie, who is now my wife. You know what, about eleven years went by where I didn't have a girlfriend—*eleven years*! That is a long time, but it in no way affected God's providing me a wife. Stephanie was the only girl I ever wanted to date; I wanted to marry her. Dating in seventh grade seemed like the thing to do, a "rite of passage"; but it really didn't accomplish much.

Dating

As fun as it is to think about spending some time with a special person, dating can be a real trap for us when we are young. That's the main reason my dad talked about setting boundaries for our lives in the last chapter. We all need to have limits in each area of our lives that will protect us emotionally and physically—and dating is no exception.

What Is Dating?

Before talking about this, first things first: How would you define dating? I want you to think about your definition of *dating* and write it down here:

_____

_____

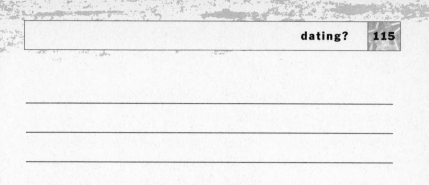

_____

_____

_____

_____

Save that definition for later. After reading this chapter your definition of dating might change, and I want you to be able to see the difference in your thinking.

So just what is dating? Some girls and guys your age had this to say:

> "Going (with the opposite sex) to a movie that I want to see."

> "For a guy and a girl to get to know each other better and have fun."

> "You go out with another person; going to the movies; holding hands."

> "Go out and have fun. Go to a bar."

Do you think those are good definitions? To be honest, some of those definitions make me wonder where the ideas are coming from! Let me take a shot at this with my definition: _Dating is when a boy and girl who like each other spend time together._ That is all it takes.

Did you think that just spending time with a girl or boy was considered dating? Probably not.

Now with my definition I do not mean that just because you hang out with somebody you like that you are "boyfriend and girlfriend." Rather, you are getting to know the other person within a dating relationship.

Why Date?

What is the purpose of dating anyway? Now that we've got a "working" definition for dating, let's see what some other people about your age had to say on the purpose of dating.

"I don't really see any purpose in dating."

"To have fun and to get to know somebody better."

"Getting to know a person better and spending more time with them so maybe you might be with them later in life."

"Getting to know people better by yourselves, not with a group."

"Mainly just to have fun."

"To find the person you might want to marry later if you are older."

Wow! There are some really good answers in that group. "Having fun with someone, getting to know them better, finding a marriage partner"—those answers are right on target. I think the ultimate purpose of dating is to find the person God is intending you to spend the rest of your life with—a husband or a wife.

> The **ultimate** **purpose of dating is** **to find the person** **God is intending** **you to spend the** **rest of your life** **with—a husband or** **a wife.**

This purpose raises the importance of dating beyond just having fun. Dating is a pretty big deal—it is a privilege and a responsibility. If you think about it, dating to find the person you are to marry means that someone who is just a teenager probably should not be dating at all. When I was thirteen I wasn't ready to take on the responsibility of getting married and providing for another person! Give me a break—I still needed a lot of help from my own parents to just keep myself together and on the right path!

This really explains why many teenagers don't have good experiences dating. This may sound kind of harsh, but I believe that young people need to grow and become mature during their teenage years. Dating relationships usually create problems; we end up hurting another person or getting hurt ourselves.

What Age to Date?

This leads us to the next big question: How old should you be to date? Let's see how some others answered:

"Fourteen or fifteen, maybe thirteen."

"I don't know."

"I think thirteen to go as a steady partner, but I think fourteen or fifteen as a date to the movies or out to dinner."

"I think at least sixteen because then you can drive. It won't be like, 'Hey, my mom and I will pick you up at six.'"

"It depends on what your parents think."

"About sixty-five."

Pretty interesting, huh? Did you notice that many of the people picked an age that's pretty near to your age now? Does that make you kind of excited? Wow, in a few short years, or even months, you might actually go with someone of the opposite sex on a date! You are growing up!

In my family my parents did not think there was a particular age at which their children should be allowed to date—it wasn't an automatic deal that when the clock struck midnight on your sixteenth birthday you could run out of the house, jump in a car, and drive to pick up a girlfriend and go out on a date alone. Rather, my parents believed that the most important dating issues were the maturity and character of the person who wanted to date.

When I was younger I wasn't so sure I agreed with Mom and

Dad on that theory, but now I do. I think you are ready for dating when you can act responsibly alone with the opposite sex, which means treating the other person with respect, having good manners, being able to engage in conversation, and being firmly in control of your emotions and physical urges.

At what age does that maturity come? Again, there is no way I could tell you without knowing you. So that's why God gave you a mom and dad—the two people in the world who really know what's up with you. Take advantage of their wisdom. My challenge to you is to wait until they give you the thumbs-up as to when you can start dating. You will not regret waiting, I promise you.

> You are **ready** for **dating** when you can act **responsibly alone** with the **opposite sex.**

rebecca's turn

When Should You Date?

My parents never set a concrete time when I could start dating. I don't remember hearing, "When you are sixteen you can date." I do remember hearing, "When you are mature enough, then you can date."

When I was in eighth grade there was a boy I liked and he liked me. We wanted to date, so I asked my parents. My mom and dad told me that they would let me date this boy if I flossed my teeth, brushed my teeth, and wore my orthodontic headgear every night for the longest time—I think it was six months! So I did what they asked, and finally we had their permission to date. I remember it was September of my ninth-grade year.

We called it "going together." My mom would always say, "Well, where are you going?" I would answer, "We're not going anywhere. We're just hanging out." Sometimes we would go to a high school football or basketball game and hang out there. Or we would ask our parents to take us to play miniature golf with some other couples. Or we would hang out at my house and watch a movie. My parents encouraged me to bring my friends home and hang out or watch movies there.

There wasn't that much pressure to be together a lot because you really did not have time. You were in school from 8 a.m. until almost 4 p.m., and after that I had homework and dinner. Weekends were the only time we could really hang out. Hanging out on a school night was just out of the question.

I don't regret the relationship I had with him, and I can proudly say that we are great friends now.

Whom to Date?

Another important question to think about is: What kind of person should you date? Here are more responses from some of your peers:

"He has to be cute."

"She has to be nice to other people."

"He has to be nice and funny."

"Understanding and thoughtful and remember things like holidays, birthdays, and stuff like that."

A follow-up question was, "How do you define *cute?*"

"Okay. Good-looking, perfect eyes, good hair, knows what to wear."

I will spend some more time later answering this question, but I wish someone had mentioned the most important quality about any person you would want to date: He or she needs to be a person who has given Jesus Christ first place in life. The most important quality is not how the other person looks, but whether or not he or she knows and walks with Jesus Christ.

A second requirement is that the person have good character—as determined by your parents! Are you willing to let your parents evaluate a potential date like that? If you said yes, that's a good sign that you are thinking right and becoming mature.

What I am getting at with these questions and answers is how important it is to have relationships that honor Jesus Christ. Remember how Colossians 1:18 says that Jesus Christ came "to have first place in everything"? Well, you know what? That means He came to have first place in all the boy-girl stuff too.

> It just is not good to **awaken** your love before it is **ready** for **the real deal.**

We wouldn't want it any other way, would we? God is for us, not against us! He wants us to enjoy ourselves. God is a loving Father who has promised to give us good gifts. Jesus said, "If you then, being evil, know how to give good gifts to your children, how much more shall your Father who is in heaven give what is good to those who ask Him!" (Matt. 7:11). You can be sure that among those good gifts will be some great relationships for you with boys and girls.

A Plan for Great Dating

Because our family has six children, over the years my parents have come up with some really good ideas on dating—even though at the time my brother and sisters were not always too crazy about them. At any rate, here are some of the "Rainey Dating Dos and Don'ts" that I think will help you and your parents come up with a great dating plan.

Dating Dos and Don'ts

Do take your time. There's no need to be in a big hurry to have a boyfriend or girlfriend. By boyfriend or girlfriend, I mean having a one-on-one, exclusive dating relationship. Regardless of what you call it—"going out" or "going steady"— exclusive dating ought to be saved for a time when you are older and more mature. Most young men and women start looking for love before they can handle it. It just is not good to awaken your love before it is ready for the real deal. Remember, the ultimate point of dating is a commitment to love and care for another person in the form of marriage. Dating is a fun but serious activity.

Don't be selfish. Many friends I knew who started dating kind of early before they were really mature seemed to focus way too much on their own needs. Two people can end up using one another just to satisfy selfish desires. A guy may want a cute girl on his arm to make him look cool or so that he can brag about her to the guys in the locker room. A girl may want a guy's attention so she will have a boyfriend just like all of her friends do. Going out with a certain guy may make her feel wanted or part of a popular clique.

Do serve others. I think a more mature way to learn how to know others and get along with them is to serve them. That is the way Jesus Christ has called us to live.

> A more **mature** way to learn how **to know others** and get along with them is to **serve them.**

Here's what Philippians 2:3–4 says on this topic: "Do nothing from selfishness or empty conceit, but with humility of mind let each of you regard one another as more important than himself; do not merely look out for your own personal interests, but also for the interests of others."

Did you catch the theme of those verses? We are told directly to put others ahead of ourselves and not be selfish. Instead of always thinking about how we can get that *special someone* to like us, why not just try to be a good friend to a lot of people—and let God in His time set us up with someone to love? If you can begin to learn how to be selfless in your friendships and other relationships, you will be way ahead of just about everyone else later on when you get married.

Do watch your heart. We've mentioned this before, but it's worth repeating: "Watch over your heart with all diligence, for from it flow the springs of life" (Prov. 4:23). One of the ways to apply that verse is to guard your heart from romantic love until you are ready to marry. If you will let them, your parents can help you guard your heart. The media constantly bombards you with the message that *you need to be in love*. Advertising, magazines, movies, the Internet, music, and television will all encourage you to establish a romantic relationship with a guy or girl. But don't listen to these messages; instead listen to your parents and guard your heart.

I remember when I first became a

teenager that many of my friends starting pairing off and "going out." I felt a lot of pressure to have a girlfriend. But my mom and dad really understood what I needed, which was time to grow up and know exactly what I wanted in a girl. I am glad that, for the most part, I guarded my heart. It was hard at times, but if I would have listened to all the "voices" from the media and my friends, then I might have really made some poor choices.

Don't missionary date. Sometimes a young guy or girl will really like someone who turns out not to be a Christian. Rather than just say, "I'd better not date that person," they get the idea in their head that they can rescue their friend who is headed down a wrong path. That's called missionary dating, and it's a very bad idea because it usually doesn't work. You know what? Let someone of the same sex redirect the path of someone who does not know Jesus. You pray for the person and encourage him or her. But don't date. This is trouble. I want to encourage you to pray for your friend who needs help. But don't think that by dating this person you can straighten him out. You are asking for trouble.

Do have many guy and girl friends. One of the problems with exclusive dating is that except for marriage there isn't a lot of good that can come out of it. Let's say some good guy-girl friends start going out and then begin dating each other exclusively. That's about all they do—just hang out with one another. The guy loses all his friends who are guys and the girl begins to neglect her friends who are girls. Before long all they have is one another. That really isn't healthy in junior high or even high school. Who wants to have just one good friend?

And if you spend a lot of time alone with that "good friend," the trap of sexual temptation can become very powerful. Really, how many good things can happen when a young man and woman spend a lot of time together alone?

Don't touch. Stay away from physical stuff in dating. We have already discussed this at length in previous chapters, but I want to really lay it on the line here: Reserve for later in marriage all the touching that leads to stirring of sexual feelings in a relationship. I've seen so many of my friends start out with a good relationship, but then the hugging and kissing and touchy-touchy started. They fell right into the trap. Some of my friends messed up and made some mistakes that they really regret now that they are married. I promise—you will never be sorry if you save your sexual intimacy for marriage. It pays to wait.

Do talk. About the most important thing you can learn now is how to talk to a boy or girl. It's fun to learn more about another person—what the other person thinks, makes her laugh, makes him happy, makes her mad. Talking is very important in relationships and especially marriage. You can start practicing now—it's cool.

Do group date. That means you hang out with a lot of different people. It's fun and safe. You get to know people, you develop lots of different kinds of relationships, you learn how to relate to each other and what you like and dislike in other people. A group situation takes away a lot of the risks, like being alone with the opposite sex and having to share too many personal things about yourself with someone who has no long-term commitment to you. Besides, when I was young, I was not ready for a heavy commitment to a girl. I needed to grow up first.

In my memory the teens who focused on group situations had more fun than those who dated exclusively. They didn't pair off; instead they learned how to get along with a lot of people and made many great buddies and friends. Some of them are friends for life because they learned how to hang out with a good group of people.

Remember when I talked about the herd? Well, group dating gives you a great opportunity to spend time with the right herd, a group of good peers who are looking for wholesome fun that honors Jesus Christ.

Do enjoy your teen years. As you move into the teenage years, you are going to be amazed at how many of your friends seem desperate to have a boyfriend or a girlfriend. It's the "thing to do" because without one, you are not a total person or something. That's ridiculous! Have fun while you can. There are a lot bigger choices and opportunities ahead of you than finding a boyfriend or girlfriend right now.

No doubt I could list many more dating dos and don'ts that have been tried out in our family. But this list is plenty to get you started. I'm sure your parents will have a few more of their own to add anyway!

How Do You Define Dating Now?

Now that you have read this chapter and thought about what I've said, take a look at the definition of dating you wrote earlier in this chapter. Have any of your ideas about dating changed? If they have, write your new definition of dating here.

_____

_____

_____

_____

_____

No matter the wording of your dating definition, Jesus Christ must be the center of your life. Let me encourage you not to let your perspective of dating get blown all out of proportion. After that early experience in junior high, I waited a lot of years to have a girlfriend! Not everyone will do that—certainly not everyone in my family has. You may choose to do some dating in your teen years, and that's cool. I think you probably will agree with me, though, when I say that dating is *not* the most important thing in life during your teenage years. If you will decide now on what your dating values will be in the future, you will save yourself and others much heartache.

Invite your parents to talk about this topic with you. Ask them what they learned about dating. Their ideas will be very beneficial. Let them help you clarify the right path for you to walk when it comes to dating. Ask them to help you stay out of the traps by pointing out where they are. And honor their wishes and defer to their authority over you. This is how God planned it so that your life will be a success.

Someday you will meet that special someone who will love you for the rest of your life. By having the right ideas on dating, and trusting your parents and God for insight and help, you can have the relationship of your dreams. Hold on to your standards and your convictions—don't let anyone convince you to drop them even for a moment. You will never regret giving Jesus Christ first place in everything.

rebecca's turn

Wait to Date?

I think my parents were right on target concerning dating. I can see the point of dating in college, because you are mature enough to prepare for marriage. But when you are in junior high and high school, you are not ready to get married. The only reason to date is for fun. If you could never see yourself marrying that person, then what is the point?

If you are dating just for fun now, then you know one of you is going to get hurt in the end. Why go through that? Because of peer pressure? Would you jump off a cliff and hurt yourself just because others were doing it too?

If you are a preteen or even a teenager, I would encourage you to wait to date until you are older. Believe me, I learned the painful way! When you are young, it's so much more fun not to have to worry about the opposite sex and whether they like you or not. And there are a lot of other fun things to do, such as getting to know the people in your school or having fun with your girl or guy friends.

Extra Stuff

KEY SCRIPTURE

Philippians 2:3–4: "Do nothing from selfishness or empty conceit, but with humility of mind let each of you regard one another as more important than himself; do not merely look out for your own personal interests, but also for the interests of others."

QUESTIONS

1. What does dating mean to most of your friends?

2. What would you say is the purpose of dating?

3. At what age do you think you would like to start dating?

4. What kind of person should you date—what qualities will you look for in the other person when you start dating?

PRAYER

Dear God, I am grateful that my parents have taken the interest and time to discuss dating with me. Help us to continue to talk often about this topic in the months and years ahead. I know I have much to learn and need their wisdom and Yours. In Jesus' name, Amen.

extreme life

by dennis rainey

Do you ever watch those extreme sports shows on TV? The ones where people jump off the side of a mountain on snow skis, or rock climb thousands of feet with their bare hands, or leap off a cliff in a hang glider and sail out over the ocean, risking the wind bashing them against the rocks at any second?

Most of us will never try a sport that extreme, and even if we did, it probably would just be a hobby—not a lifelong career.

But there is an exciting way to live that is very extreme and you can do it "24/7" the rest of your life. It's called following Jesus, and the best time to learn the basics of this extreme way of living is right now—when you are young.

Have you seen what happens to some older people? As many people age, the harder it is for them to change and be really

adventurous or "extreme" about new ways of thinking or living. Unfortunately, often this is even true

There is an
exciting way to
live that is very
extreme . . .
It's called
following Jesus.

about their walk with God.

So this is *the time* in your life to
decide how you will respond to God. I
urge you to get extreme in your obe-
dience and desire to do His will. That
means you need to make some decisions and choices *now* that will help get
you to where you want to go.

If you want an exciting, extreme kind of life that honors God
and blesses you and others, I want you to read the following
words carefully and sign your name to the promise statements.
Make sure you have a pen before you start. If you are not comfortable signing some of these, then I want you to wait until you
can wholeheartedly "sign on the dotted line" with full confidence that you intend to keep your word. This is not a test, and
no one needs to see what you write in this book. Just be honest
with yourself and with God.

Are you ready? Here goes!

Extreme Life Promises

1. I will make Jesus both Savior and Lord of my life and serve
   and love Him joyfully with all my heart, soul, and mind.

_____   _____

Signature   Date

2. I will honor God by obeying my parents and having a good attitude toward them.

_____   _____

Signature   Date

3. I will stand up for what is right even if my friends and others disagree or make fun of me.

_____   _____

Signature   Date

4. I will guard my heart and mind by not watching unclean movies or pornography or listening to music with words of violence or sex.

_____   _____

Signature   Date

5. I will not play computer games that emphasize sex and violence and will not use the Internet to look at pornography or participate in bad or dangerous chat rooms.

_____   _____

Signature   Date

6. I will not smoke, drink alcohol, or use drugs.

_____   _____

Signature   Date

7. I will not make fun of other boys or girls as their bodies change during adolescence.

_____   _____

Signature   Date

8. I will honor members of the opposite sex by dressing appropriately and modestly, by not flirting, by not being physically aggressive, and by keeping my sexual desires under control.

_____   _____

Signature   Date

9. I will not date until my parents say I am ready emotionally, physically, and spiritually.

_____   _____

Signature   Date

10. Based on my answers to the chart shown on the next page, I have decided that I will not go beyond _____ [fill in the activity] with someone of the opposite sex before marriage.

_____   _____

Signature   Date

11. I will remain pure and keep my sex gift for my spouse in marriage.

_____   _____

Signature   Date

12. As I grow up I will protect unborn life myself by not having an abortion or by encouraging a friend to have an abortion.

_____   _____

Signature   Date

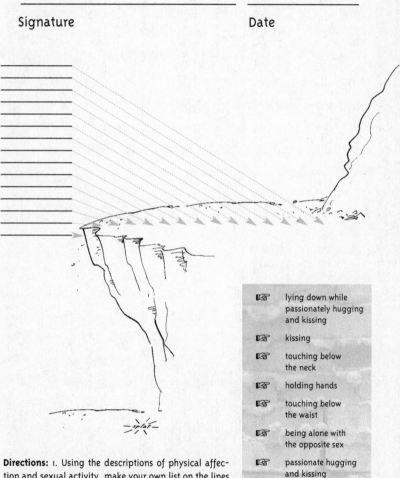

☞ lying down while passionately hugging and kissing

☞ kissing

☞ touching below the neck

☞ holding hands

☞ touching below the waist

☞ being alone with the opposite sex

☞ passionate hugging and kissing

☞ intercourse

☞ hugs

☞ taking clothes off

Directions: 1. Using the descriptions of physical affection and sexual activity, make your own list on the lines provided of activities that go from least dangerous (by the cliff) to the most dangerous (off the cliff). 2. Place an "x" on the cliff (next to the arrow point for that activity) that shows how far you think the average teenager today goes in expressing physical affection to someone of the opposite sex.

I sincerely hope that you were able to sign your name to all of those promises, and I'm sorry if you now have writer's cramp!

God bless you as you begin this exciting part of what I know will be your "extreme life for God." You will love being a teenager!

SPECIAL OFFER! If you would like a certificate that includes all of the above statements with one spot for you to sign and date, go to www.familylife.com/preteen on the Internet and follow the instructions. You can download, print, sign, and frame the certificate. Hang it on a wall where you will often see these important promises you have made!

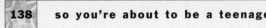 **rebecca's turn**

Decide in Advance

Even as I started junior high I saw that kids were making choices and you had to quickly decide what kind of group you would hang out with. Some of the people I had known in elementary school decided to drink and smoke, but I didn't. My morals were different from theirs, so we really didn't have much in common anymore. I remember them pressuring me, but I was never really that tempted to give in. In my mind there really was no choice. I didn't think, *Should I or should I not?* I already knew. The answer was no. That stuff is gross anyway.

My parents really helped me stand strong.

The people I hung out with in junior high knew me and my morals, so later in high school they really didn't pressure me. They knew I was going to say no. Sure, they asked me to parties and asked me to go out, but I knew my parents would always be behind me. I'm thankful for Mom and Dad, because I didn't have that many close friends who were supporting me in making the right decisions.

If I had not decided ahead of time what my choices would be, would I have made bad decisions? Probably so.

Use the following pages
to write out your thoughts
on becoming a teenager—
or you can just use this
space to doodle.

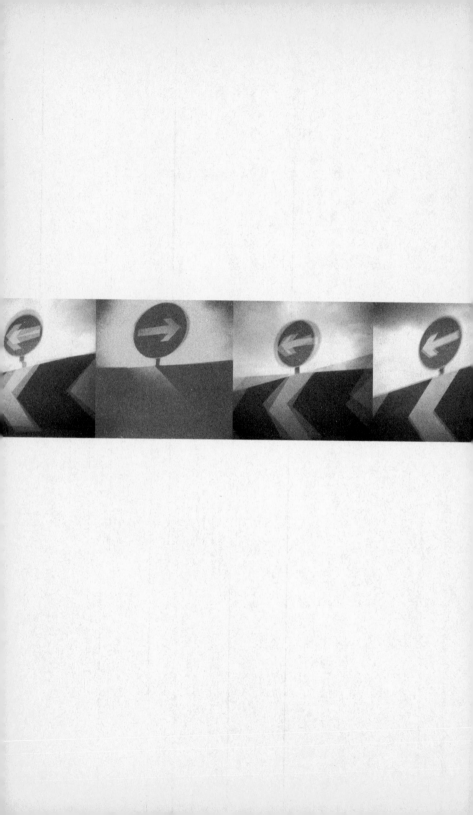

A Passport to Purity Weekend

Some parents find it helpful to schedule a special "rite of passage" weekend to review the topics covered in this book in a concentrated, memorable way. To help facilitate such an experience, FamilyLife has developed a package called *Passport to Purity*. This boxed kit includes:

Audio Tour: Five topics are discussed on audiotape by Dennis and Barbara Rainey. Drama and music are used to make the content captivating to a preteen. A special instruction tape for parents is included.

Tour Guide: This manual for parents explains how to prepare for and conduct the weekend. It includes plenty of tips on meals, projects, and fun activities.

Adventure Journal: This manual for the preteen contains a note-taking outline for each session and "make up your mind" discussion questions. Creative illustrative art aids content comprehension.

My Passport: A unique document to help the preteen solidify the commitment made to purity. Both parent and preteen sign the passport in a special ceremony that concludes the weekend.

Although this material ideally is presented to a preteen, *Passport to Purity* is suitable for use with young teens as well.

If you are interested in more information on *Passport to Purity*, go to www.familylife.com/preteen or call 1-800-FL TODAY.

Acknowledgments

Barbara and Dennis would like to thank:

Our children, Samuel and Rebecca, who injected so much energy and fun into this project—congratulations on your first book;

Bruce Nygren for his advice, commitment to excellence, and sharp editing pen—thanks for your ministry to the next generation through this book;

The always awesome team at FamilyLife—Clark Hollingsworth, John Majors, Janet Logan, Cherry Tolleson, Mark Whitlock, David Boehi, and Ben Colter;

Our panel of preteen readers who offered superb advice and encouragement—Logan Beck, Brian Cooper, Rebecca Daggett, Jared Elmquist, Stephen Hedges, David Lindahl, Jessica Russo, and Samarra Simmons;

Our faithful colaborers at Thomas Nelson Publishers: Brian Hampton, Kyle Olund, Lori Lynch, and Mike Hyatt. Thanks for your labor of love in this strategic resource for preteens.

About the Authors

Dennis Rainey is the cofounder of the FamilyLife Ministry and the author, coauthor, or general editor of many books, including *Parenting Today's Adolescent*, *Starting Your Marriage Right*, *We Still Do*, *Building Your Mate's Self-Esteem*, and *The Tribute and the Promise*. Dennis also cohosts the award-winning nationally syndicated *FamilyLife Today* radio program.

Barbara Rainey has served on the staff of Campus Crusade for Christ for twenty-six years. She is the coauthor or general editor of several books, including *A Mother's Legacy*, which she wrote with her oldest daughter, Ashley Rainey Escue. Barbara has written numerous articles on family-related topics and speaks with Dennis at various conferences.

The Raineys have six children and live near Little Rock, Arkansas.

Samuel Rainey is the graphics production manager for a company in Franklin, Tennessee. He and his wife, Stephanie, welcomed into this world their first child, Peterson, in March 2003.

Rebecca Rainey graduated in May 2003 from the University of Arkansas, where she majored in English with an emphasis on creative writing.